BUDDHISM AND SCIENCE

Buddhism and Science

Edited by

BUDDHADASA P. KIRTHISINGHE

MOTILAL BANARSIDASS PUBLISHERS
PRIVATE LIMITED • DELHI

First Edition: Delhi, 1984
Reprint: Delhi, 1993, 1996

ISBN: 81-208-0803-7

Also available at:

MOTILAL BANARSIDASS
41 U.A. Bungalow Road, Jawahar Nagar, Delhi 110 007
8, Mahalaxmi Chamber, Warden Road, Mumbai 400 026
120 Royapettah High Road, Mylapore, Madras 600 004
Sanas Plaza, Subhash Nagar, Pune 411 002
16 St. Mark's Road, Bangalore 560 001
8 Camac Street, Calcutta 700 017
Ashok Rajpath, Patna 800 004
Chowk, Varanasi 221 001

PRINTED IN INDIA

BY JAINENDRA PRAKASH JAIN AT SHRI JAINENDRA PRESS,
A-45 NARAINA, PHASE I, NEW DELHI 110 028
AND PUBLISHED BY NARENDRA PRAKASH JAIN FOR
MOTILAL BANARSIDASS PUBLISHERS PRIVATE LIMITED,
BUNGALOW ROAD, DELHI 110 007

DEDICATED

to

the Venerable Bhikkhu Vipassi of Sri Lanka

Chairman of the Hospital Welfare Fund of the All-Ceylon Buddhist Congress, whose dedicated services to assist the needy, sick, feeble and old people are too well known.

He works on the golden traditions set by his Great Teacher—the Buddha himself—who stated, while nursing a sick monk, "He who nurses the sick, nurseth me." This is said to have influenced some nations to build hospitals in Buddhist Asia from India—Sri Lanka to Japan from the 3rd century B.C.

May we strengthen his hands by contributing all income from this book to continue to fulfil his noble and cherished ideals.

CONTENTS

FOREWORD

We do not generally speak about religion and science in the same or amiable context. In fact, science and religion are, rightly or wrongly, still being considered as opposite poles.

When, therefore, Buddhism, which is very often and somewhat erroneously regarded as a religion instead of an ethical way of life and mode of thinking, is compared in its underlying philosophical and metaphysical teachings with the concepts of modern physics and biology, most people will assume a skeptical attitude. They may refer to such attempts graciously as a mistake, and ungraciously as absurdity.

Both sides are wrong, wrong in their assumptions and wrong in their conclusions. All the more astounding it is that few will raise their eyebrows when some of the intellectual and scientific elite of this 20th century profess to see no difficulty in citing Western religious scriptures as authority even though scientifically, sociologically and ethically we have far transcended the old traditional contentions and standards. In science this is most obvious and we need only to refer to the creation stories. In social theories few would go along with the theocratic, patriarchial and kin-dominated family system. Our moral sensibilities also have improved in many areas, such as the treatment of animals and the obsolescence of words like righteousness and justification. The articles included in this book suggest that the Buddha announced some 25 centuries ago principles which we can glean from an examination of the latest contributions by experts in biology, physics, psychology and psychiatry. If these were haphazard comparisons, our position might still be polite aloofness. But the remarkable fact is that if reduced to general principles, many statements in the Buddhist scriptures can be brought in line with modern scientific theories and hypotheses.

Perhaps one reason is that Buddhist thinking has always enjoyed the greatest freedom untrammelled by dogmatism and authority of any kind, not even that of the Buddha himself. We have his words in the Kalama Sutta which should be given into the hands of any who write and pronounce judgment on Buddhism.

This collection of articles edited by Dr. Buddhadasa P. Kirthisinghe, a devoted and knowledgeable Buddhist and a scientist in the field of microbiology, should not only prove interesting, but thought-provoking, and create a desire to pry more deeply into the many-faceted Buddhist literature.

Kurt F. Leidecker
President
Buddhist Centre of America
Professor Emeritus
Philosophy and Religion
Mary Washington College

306 Caroline Street
Fredericksburg, Va
U.S.A. 22401

PREFACE

When the 1966 World Buddhism Wesak Annual brought out my essay on "Buddhism, Biology and Exobiology," the Venerable Nyanaponika Maha Nayaka Thera, Editor of the Buddhist Publications Society in Kandy, Sri Lanka, encouraged me to enlarge on the theme and show the close relationship between Buddhism and science in other fields also. The present volume is the result.

I am particularly grateful to a few scientists and other scholars who have made their essays available for inclusion in this collection of essays. Dr. Shanti Tayal, a clinical psychologist, contributed "The Buddha's Middle Way and Western Psychotherapy," Dr. Loo Yung Tsung contributed "Buddhism and Nuclear Physics," and Gerald Du Pré of Great Britain his 8 essays published in the *Middle Way*, the Journal of the Buddhist Society of London, England, on various aspects of Buddhism and science.

Also included is an essay on Biochemistry and Buddhism by Dr. Aung Thein; an essay on Buddhism and science by the late Professor K. N. Jayatilleke and furthermore, an essay on the science and philosophy of Aniccam by the Venerable Bhikkhu Nanajivako, both of Sri Lanka; an essay on the relationship between Buddhism and modern science by Robert F. Spencer and between Buddhism and Cosmology by Frederick M. Davis. The last two authors are from the U.S.A.

It is hoped that it would be evident from a reading of these diverse essays that Buddhist philosophy blends well with science in its various fields. Just as Buddhist views in regard to the universe do not clash even with the most modern concepts, similarly Buddhist ideas on philosophy do not clash with the concepts in the various religions, provided they are analyzed correctly.

It is a pleasant duty to acknowledge with thanks the help I have received in this compilation. Despite heavy duties the Venerable Nyanaponika, Editor, Buddhist Publications Society, Kandy, Sri Lanka, Mr. Gerald Du Pré of Great Britain and

Dr. Kurt F. Leidecker, President of the Friends of Buddhism, read the manuscript carefully and made many valuable suggestions. Miss Betty M. Knight and Mrs. Eileene M. Barham of England, assisted in the typing of the manuscript. To all of them, my heartfelt thanks.

Buddhadasa P. Kirthisinghe

American Buddhist Academy
689 Columbus Ave.
New York City 10025

INTRODUCTION
BUDDHISM AND SCIENCE

by

THE EDITOR

If we scan the history of Western civilization beginning in Greece, we will be impressed by the fact that not only have there been many wars and tragic conflicts in which thousands of humans were sacrificed, but that many of these wars were not fought for economic reasons alone. Quite a few were brought about by a conflict of opinion as to the nature, the origin and the destiny of man and the world. These opinions, again, had their origin in religion.

The dominant religion in the West has been Christianity. Hence we can safely hold it responsible for so many wars and much bloodshed. For Christianity became, by the fourth century C. E., the dominant ideological force in the Western world. It prescribed what had to be believed and what had to be accepted as truth.

Now, since all dogmas of the Christian Church are based on the belief in revelation and revelation is laid down in the books of the Bible, whatever the Bible said was considered as the absolute truth. This truth is not to be questioned under threat of hell-fire and damnation.

Thus, it is clear that the ultimate basis of Christianity, which itself claims to be the basis of Western civilization, is the belief in the revealed word of God, while God is the necessary condition of all belief whatsoever, in the Christian sense.

Science, however, is based on other presuppositions. Science observes, describes, establishing the truth on ocular demonstration and verification by experiment which anyone may undertake without the least faith in ultimate results. Faith has no place in science at all, only honest application of an objective method and adherence to its results. It is, thus, seen that science is a human endeavour quite different from religion as conceived by Christianity which is based on faith and belief, and belief of a special kind at that. For the beliefs of all other religions are summarily rejected as erroneous.

Moreover, if a scientist makes an error, he is not punished for it here or in the next world. But if an error is made in Christianity, it has extremely severe consequences which are not confined to this life. We are happy to say that much of Christianity is no longer caught up in this dogmatism which condemns all reason and difference of opinion. The major denominations of Christianity have become more lenient and tolerant. But for centuries they waged a fierce war against the very attitude of the scientist who endeavoured to find out the true nature of the world and of man, by means of reason and experiment, not by consulting an ancient book compiled by seers and mystics on the basis of intuitions and revelations. Whatever progress has been made in the Western world in science and technology, was made not because of faith and belief in the supernatural, but largely by rejecting it or being indifferent to it.

All would be well if the dogmas of religion bore any semblance to the reality which the scientist investigates. But it clearly is not so. For none of the supernatural concepts, such as a personal God, miracles, the fall of man and man's redemption, can be proved objectively, certainly not by reason. When the Church could not maintain what could not be demonstrated, or offended common sense and practical experience, it relented somewhat and refrained from persecuting the scientists who had so valiantly defended their interpretation of reality. Scientists could no longer be muzzled or burned at the stake for their "error", because reason and demonstration could no longer be denied their right to existence, especially since it led to an improvement in man's living conditions in the economic and social spheres. The Church had done nothing in this direction because faith told it that God wanted it that way—that the poor will always be with us, for instance.

There is no doubt, however, that much progress has been made in the West in every line of endeavour in the physical sphere. More progress could have been made and with less agony if religion had not interfered with scientific interpretation of reality and the world based on speculation in the supernatural realm, if it had not taken the words of the Bible in a literal sense or as the revealed word of God, as, for instance, that the world is flat, that the earth is stationary and the sun revolves around it, that it is wrong to subject natural phenomena to scientific test, and that there is no universal causation or evolution, but that special creation by a deity is the true concept. At almost every turn, religion opposed the scientist and many still call science irreligious and materialistic. Religion often blocked values and improvements in living which science tried to realise. Conditions, no matter how dire, were attributed to God who in this way put man's faith to test and tried to prepare him for a future life of happiness in heaven. The optimism of science was often condemned and a pessimistic attitude was substituted which called for man's repentance, humility, submission to the will of God, as interpreted by the Church authorities.

Over against this we have the attitude of the Buddhist who has never been hampered in his thought and action by any dogma or supernatural revelation. The Buddhist looks up to the Buddha, the Awakened or Enlightened One, who saw the misery of the world, the dire conditions under which man lives, who is ill, poor and subject to adversity and death. He wanted to make man happy, wanted to help him out of the pain and suffering which he encounters. He wanted to show him the way to *nirvāṇa* or lasting bliss.

This the Buddha did, not by requiring man to believe in a supernatural being, a God, or even in himself, though nearly perfect that he was. If a man is drowning, he does not enquire of those on the shore how deep the lake is, how cold the water is, to whom the lake belongs, etc. Similarly, a man who has been wounded by a poisoned arrow does not enquire about the kind of arrow, the type of bow, from what distance he was hit, nor any other thing of the kind. Both men want to know how to overcome the straits in which they find themselves. Anything else is extraneous and not to the point. Likewise, it is not to the point what he believes in respect of a deity, whether he created the lake, the poison, whether and when he made the earth, whether the world is eternal or not, whether it is finite or infinite. These are questions which philosophers, the Brāhmaṇas of the ancient Hindu scriptures and others interested in metaphysics, try to solve. These problems as such are not useless to think about; but if a person finds himself in a difficult situation from which he wants to disengage himself, metaphysical and theological speculations are of no avail. The Buddha did not condemn such speculations about the age of the world, the nature of creation and the like. For example, a scientist who is interested in geological formations leaves out of consideration what a physiologist has to say about the human body and its organs. When he needs such knowledge, he will apply to the physician, but not when he studies geological strata. Likewise, the man in search of happiness and peace of mind and heart will look toward those things which the Buddha said might help him to attain them. He may be a philosopher and a theologian, he may be a logician and know a great deal about metaphysical problems. But in this case he has no need of such knowledge. That does not make him an atheist, nor is his search for contentment materialistic. Thus we see that the Buddha had no quarrel with any or all persons who believe, have faith or knowledge of various sorts. His objective was to satisfy the immediate needs for overcoming pain and suffering. A physician attending on the wounds of a man does not first ask him whether or not he goes to the church. He is a physician and his job is to treat the person. So was Buddha a physician of the soul and the body and he proceeded in a scientific manner by first of all analyzing the disease.

By using the scientific method, the Buddha proved that he was, indeed, a scientist. Hence from this consideration alone it is futile to ask whether he, his followers or his statements can be considered as scientific or inimical to science. He and his followers, and the whole procedure that the Buddhists employ, are in conformity with and in the spirit of science. Hence, no quarrel could ever arise with people who accept scientific principles or make scientific discoveries. The Buddha and Buddhists welcome each scientific discovery, each new application of scientific principles, for these could never be contrary to the principles that they themselves employ.

Nevertheless, each man is selective in his experience. As such any one who is in search of a cure selects ways and means of alleviating his condition and leaves others unconsidered. It so happened that the Buddha, in overcoming misery and pain and sorrow, selected the ethical means. But even here the scientific presuppositions show through most markedly. For he bases everything on cause-effect relationships, often pointing out subtle connections which we in our haste and impatience are prone to overlook, but which psychologists, and psychoanalysts in particular, recognize.

Science is based most assuredly on analysis, that is, the scrutinizing of every phenomenon and examining every part of it and finding out how it came about. That is exactly what the Buddha did. The assumption that there is pain and sorrow and misery, and the assumption that everything, no matter what, has a cause, are the only two assumptions that the Buddha made. One is based on observation and introspection and a generalization from human experience; the other is the very life-blood of science, whether made in the East or in the West. Sharing thus the very foundation of the scientific attitude, how could the Buddha—and the Buddhists—ever quarrel with what the scientific method yields? How could they restrict the scientific method? How can they throttle it if they employ it themselves? How can they throw an anathema against science? How can they command a halt in the middle of an experiment and say: Now invoke faith and belief that has been recorded and professed by the non-scientists?

It can be safely assumed that Buddhism has never had any quarrel with science or scientists, leave alone persecuted any scientists for their findings, made them recant or burnt them at the stake. Not only are these things utterly incomprehensible to a Buddhist, who leads a moral life of non-violence, but they would be nonsensical because the Buddhist never opposed scientific methods. The fact is that in the history of Buddhism there has never been any altercations with scientists, and no war has ever been declared on science, nor has there ever been declared a holiday for science on the plea that science had, as some Western moralists and theologians assumed, gone astray and worked for ill instead of good. Science is neutral; it is man's mind and disposition which ought to be guided along ethical lines and that precisely is the function of the Buddhist teachings. Warfare beween science and Christianity ? Yes, there has been too much of it. Warfare between science and Buddhism ? Never.

Not only has there never been any warfare between Buddhism and the other religions, but Buddhism has found itself seldom in disagreement with any earnest search for truth. It has never opposed or resisted such a search, but has rather encouraged it. The legitimate question may, of course, be asked, why has there not been more science in the East since Buddhism held sway for many centuries in the countries of the Orient ? The answer is simple. There has been more science and many more scientific discoveries and technological inventions than are generally recognized. Their list is a long one, but we generally do not study Eastern civilizations from this point of view, thinking the modern Western civilization to be superior. But more significantly, the Buddhist has greater concern with peace of mind, kindness, *mettā*, compassion, *karuṇā*, and a genuine interest in the joys of others, *muditā*, than with perfecting gadgets which in themselves not only do not contribute to a lessening of sorrow and suffering in the world but are more often than not augmenting them. Just think with what precision we have developed military science and technology while our social problems are still in a sad state. We have, for instance, all the means of bringing heaven down to earth, but we fear and anticipate and are obsessed by the thought of war. On the other hand, the Buddhist, though he has not developed the technological skill to make everyone satisfied with living without drudgery, he has yet found a way to happiness and bliss. The problem of strife and warfare does not enter his mind at all. He keeps his peace, we think of preventing war.

There is, of course, an opinion in the West that it is through the terrible intellectual and emotional crises which the West has passed through in moulding its civilization, including the warfare between science and religion, that man has attained a greater stature, has matured more, has been cleansed by the agony of it all and has redeemed himself. But has he, indeed ? Has he attained a greater spirituality ? Many question it even in the West. But be this as it may, Buddhism has never contributed to agony in the world, but has always tried to alleviate it even without the sacrifice of spirituality.

Religion in the West has always assumed an authoritarian,

if not dictatorial, attitude, and so has Western science. It was natural, therefore, that the two should clash. Buddhism has never assumed the airs of authoritarianism and has not gone out of its way to avoid clashes with science. Not only this, it has not even recognized that there is a difference between it and science, which in itself would make rivalry nugatory and nonsensical. There is no reason why in this modern world these qualities of Buddhism cannot be maintained. There is even the possibility that Buddhism can contribute to modern life and society significantly by providing the ethical basis for our industrial and technological age, something which the Western religion has not been able to do because it still harbours suspicions in regard to the so-called materialistic aims of science. By making compromises, the Western religion is not sure of its own stand and principles. Of late they have been questioned so severely by the lay and church people alike. The clear-cut ethical teachings of Buddhism have clearly an advantage in that they are won analytically—that is, in the modern scientific spirit—and are not weighed down by requirements of faith or belief.

BUDDHISM AND THE SCIENTIFIC REVOLUTION

by

K. N. Jayatilleke

It is an historical fact that the scientific revolution which took its rise in the seventeenth century in the West was largely responsible for upsetting the earlier religious conception of the universe. Not only did science controvert the specific dogmas of the Western religion, but it seemed to have undermined the foundations as well as the fundamental concepts implicit in a religious outlook on things.

The new cosmology of Copernicus, Galileo and their successors altered the geocentric picture of the universe although it was pronounced to be "contrary to the Holy Scriptures". The new biology (the theory of evolution) upset the doctrines of the special creation and the fall of man. And the new psychology seemed to show that man's mind, like his physical body, worked on a pattern of causal law and that however deep one plumbed its depths, it would not be possible to discover in it an unchanging soul which governed all its activities.

But much more serious was the effect of the scientific outlook on the general religious attitude which involved a belief in a Personal God, in purpose and in the objectivity of moral values. Science made its discoveries and progressed quite comfortably on the assumption of universal causation without the necessity for teleological explanations or divine intervention. It dealt with an amoral universe indifferent to the aspirations of men. As among men, moral values, like economic values, were subjective since they were dependent on the needs and desires of men, and an ethical humanism was the best that could be hoped for. Even such an ethic need not be universal for, as anthropologists discovered, different societies seem to have followed different moral codes which suited them. Accordingly, ethical relativism was the scientific truth about the nature of moral values.

Of course there are those who still cling to the dogmas in the face of science or believe in them in a non-literal sense. But the position remains very much the same although people are no longer optimistic (after being through two world wars and in the throes of a third one) about the ability of science to usher in a brave new world of peace and plenty. It has also been granted that mechanistic explanations of the universe need not necessarily rule out teleological ones. Science too has given up the crude materialism of the eighteenth century and scientists no longer attempt to explain the universe on machine models, while some scientists have denied that strict determination holds in the sphere of the atom. But all this is still a far cry from religion.

What place would Buddhism occupy in such a context ? Are its dogmas and attitudes no better or no worse than those of any other religion ? Some Western writers on religion seem to have assumed that this was so, but if one reads through the Buddhist texts, one begins to wonder whether the scientific revolution would have at all affected religion adversely if it had taken place in the context of Early Buddhism.

I say this because I find that Early Buddhism emphasises the importance of the scientific outlook in dealing with the problems of morality and religion. Its specific 'dogmas' are said to be capable of verification. And its general account of the nature of man and the universe is one that accords with the findings of science rather than being at variance with them.

To take this last point first, we find for instance, that the Early Buddhist conception of the cosmos, is in essence similar to the modern conception of the universe. In the Pāli texts that have come down to us, we are literally told that hundreds and thousands of suns and moons, earths, and higher worlds, constitute the minor world system, that a hundred thousand times this, is the middling world system, and a hundred thousand times the middling world system, is the major world system. In modern terminology, it would seem as if a minor world system (*culanikā-loka-dhātu*) is a galaxy of which we observe about a hundred million through our best telescope. The Buddhist conception of time is equally immense.

There is, of course, no theory of biological evolution as such, mentioned in the Buddhist texts, but man and society, as well as worlds, are pictured as changing and evolving in accordance with the causal laws.

Then in psychology we find Early Buddhism regarding man as a psycho-physical unit whose 'psyche' is not a changeless soul but a dynamic continuum composed of a conscious mind as well as an unconscious, in which are stored the residua of emotionally charged memories going back to childhood as well as into past lives. Such a mind is said to be impelled to act under the influence of three types of desires—the desire for sense-gratification (*kāma-taṇhā*), the desire for self-preservation (*bhava-taṇhą̄*) and the desire for destruction (*vibhava-taṇhā*). Except for the belief in rebirth, this conception of the mind sounds very modern, and one cannot also fail to observe the parallel between the threefold desire in Buddhism and the Freudian conception of the eros, libido, and thanatos.

I have brought out these similarities not with the intention of showing that Buddhism teaches modern science, but that the scientific revolution does not have the same adverse effect on Buddhism as it had on another religious tradition.

Now let us turn to the content of Buddhism as a theory about the nature and destiny of man. First of all it holds that an honest impartial search for truth, even in matters moral and religious, is no bar to one's spiritual progress. On more than one occasion the Buddha has admonished honest seekers after the truth in the following words: "You have raised a doubt in a situation in which you ought to suspend your judgement. Do not accept anything because it is rumoured so, because it is the traditional belief, because the majority hold to it, because it is found in the scriptures, because it is the product of metaphysical argument and speculation, or after a superficial investigation of facts, or because it conforms with one's inclinations, because it is authoritative or because of the prestige value of your teacher." Critical investigation and personal verification was to be the guide to true morality and religion. "If anyone were to speak ill of me, my doctrine and my order," says the Buddha, "do not bear any ill-will towards him, be upset or perturbed at heart, for if you were to be so, it will only cause you harm. If on the other hand anyone were to speak well of me, my doctrine and my order, do not be overjoyed, thrilled or elated at heart, for if so it will only be an obstacle in your way of forming a correct judgement as to whether the qualities praised in us are real and actually found in us." A scientific outlook was thus considered necessary, not only for discovering the truly moral and religious life, but even for the continual self-examination which such a life demands.

The field of moral and religious phenomena is, again, not a realm of mystery but one in which the law of cause and effect holds. The principle of causal determination, namely, that A is the cause of B if "whenever an event A occurs, an event B occurs, and B does not occur unless A has occurred" has been laid down by the Buddha in these very terms. He further states that "he speaks only of causes and of things which arise from causes". Thus all phenomena, including the moral and spiritual experiences (with the sole exception of Nirvāṇa which is not a conditioned phenomenon), are said to be conditioned by causal laws. Such laws are classified according to their sphere of operation as physical laws (*utuniyama*), biological laws (*vejaniyama*), psychological laws (*cittaniyama*) and moral and spiritual laws (*dhamma-niyama*).

Now there are three laws which are said to govern the life and destiny of the individual. They are the law of continuity, which makes for the persistence of individuality (*bhava*), the law of moral retribution (*karma*) whereby morally good acts tend to result in pleasant consequences and morally evil acts in unpleasant consequences for the individual, and finally, the law of causal genesis (*paṭiccasamuppāda*) which is intended to explain the above two laws.

The law of continuity, popularly known as rebirth, ensures the persistence of the dynamic unconscious of the individual with the death of the physical body. If this unconscious is not attuned to higher worlds by the moral and spiritual development of the individual, it is said generally to persist in the spirit-sphere (*petti-visaya*) as a discarnate spirit, and subsequently get reborn as a human. Critics of Buddhism often suggest that this theory of rebirth is dogmatically accepted or taken for granted in Buddhism, but a careful study of the texts would show that this is not the case.

Buddhism arose at a time when there was intense speculation on the problem of survival. There were also several schools of materialism, all of which denied survival altogether, and there were the sceptics who merely doubted the possibility of survival. Even experiments such as the weighing of the body immediately before and after death were performed in order to discover any evidence of survival. One of the materialist theories, mentioned and dismissed by the Buddha, was that consciousness was a by-product of the material elements being mixed up in certain proportions to form the organic body "in the same way in which the red colour is produced by suitable mixtures of betel, arecanut and lime" (none of which is red). Several such materialistic theories, as well as a number of one-life-after-death-theories, some of which held that the soul was conscious after death, others that it was unconscious (but existing), and yet others that it was super-conscious after death, are examined and disposed of by the Buddha. The theory of rebirth is offered as one capable of being verified by developing the faculty of seeing our former births, a potentiality which is said to be within the reach of all of us.

Rebirth is therefore not a dogma to be accepted on faith but an hypothesis capable of being scientifically verified. Evidence available for rebirth today is roughly of two sorts. There is the spontaneous evidence of numerous people from both East and West who have claimed to remember their past lives, in some cases the memories have been confirmed by further investigation (e.g., the case of Shanti Devi, *The Illustrated Weekly of India*, December 15, 1935; the case of Nellie Horster, *Milwaukee Sentinel*, September 25, 1892). There is also the more reliable and abundant evidence of psychiatrists and psychologists who have discovered that under hypnotic trance the subject's memories can be traced back not only to childhood but to prior earth lives as well; in some cases the facts have been verified (e.g. A. de Rochas, *Les Vies Successives*, Bibliotheque Charcomac, Paris; Ralph Shirley, *The Problem of Rebirth*, Rider & Co., London; Professor Theodore Flournoy, *Des Inde a la planet March*; Professor Charles E. Cory, "A Divided Self", in *Journal of Abnormal Psychology*, Vol. XIV, 1919).

The law of moral retribution or karma as taught in Buddhism has also been criticised on the grounds that it amounts to fatalism. This again is due to ignorance of the Buddhist teaching. Causation in Buddhism is carefully distinguished by the Buddha, on the one hand from Strict Determinism, and on the other from Indeterminism. The Buddha argues that if everything was determined, then there would be no free will and no moral or spiritual life would be possible and we would be mere slaves of the past; on the other hand, if everything was indetermined (*adhicca-samuppanna*) or fortuitous, then again the moral and spiritual life would not be possible, for the cultivation of moral and spiritual values would not result in moral and spiritual growth. According to the Buddha, it is because the world is so constituted that everything is not strictly determined or completely indetermined that the religious life is possible and desirable.

In order to explain rebirth and karma, some of the Upaniṣadic thinkers who accepted these doctrines had recourse to the concept of *ātman* or a changeless soul. The individual continued to be the same because he had a permanent soul which was the agent of all the actions as well as the experiencer of their fruits. The Buddha was quick to see that such metaphysical entities explained nothing and that it was meaningless to assert or deny an unverifiable entity. He therefore rejected the concept of soul, while maintaining the doctrine of the observable continuity of individuality, and explained the above two laws of continuity and moral retribution in terms of all the verifiable phenomenal factors which determine the continued genesis and growth of the individual. This is too elaborate to be set out in detail here. In brief, it describes how the individual is conditioned by his psychological past (going back to past lives which set the general tone of his character) and the genetical constitution of his body derived from his parents. The individual continues to act in and react to his environment, accumulating the experiences of this life in his evolving consciousness (*saṃvattanika-viññāṇa*) which continues after the death of the body, if the threefold desire in it be still active.

Personal and direct knowledge of the operation of these three laws constitutes the threefold knowledge (*tisso vijjā*) which the Buddha and his disciples claimed to have. Awareness of the fact and the way in which one is being conditioned is said to result in one's ceasing to be conditioned, a state which corresponds to the attainment of the unconditioned and supreme felicity of *Nirvāṇa*. This is salvation in Buddhism, which is literally, salvation from the bondage of finite and conditioned existence.

Strictly, *Nirvāṇa* is said to be beyond description or conception, the reason given being that it is a state so radically different from the type of existent things which we can conceive of that no meaningful description or definition of it can be given in conceptual terms. It is asserted that to say that one 'exists' in *Nirvāṇa* is wrong, for existence is a concept that applies to phenomenal things and has reference to space and time. *Nirvāṇa* is "timeless, in that one cannot speak of it as being in the past, present or future", is not located in space and is not causally conditioned unlike all phenomenal things: but it is claimed to be equally wrong to say that one "does not exist" in *Nirvāṇa* since this implies a state of oblivion and annihilation. Nevertheless, both positive as well as negative descriptions are given though they are not to be taken as exact definitions, as *Nirvāṇa* is "beyond the scope of logic".

Negatively, *Nirvāṇa* is the absence of all unhappiness. All phenomenal existence is said to be infected with unhappiness; we are unhappy either because we experience mental or physical pain and have forebodings for the future, or because the pleasant experiences that we have are insecure and never lasting. This is to take a realistic view of life even in the face of the fact that, as the Buddha says, "human beings enjoy on the whole more pleasant experiences than unpleasant ones", and therefore it would not be correct to call it pessimism since it has nothing to do with wishful thinking. Positively, *Nirvāṇa* is described as a state of "supreme felicity" (*paramam sukham*).

The way of salvation is described as an eightfold path in which the first step is that of right understanding and living in accordance with the true philosophy of life, and as a result having right aspirations, right speech, right actions, right mode of living, and right mindfulness, culminating in the growth of religious joy and the spiritual and intuitive awareness of right meditation or contemplation. The full fruit of right contemplation, however, can be reaped only by those giving up the active social life for the contemplative life. This meditative life is characterised by the stages of personal mystical consciousness (*rūpa-jhāna*) and impersonal mystical consciousness (*arūpa-jhāna*) culminating in the attainment of *Nirvāṇa*. With the growth of his mind and spirit, there are said to emerge in the individual, certain faculties latent in him such as telepathy and clairvoyance and the ability to see his past lives. These cognitive faculties, as explained earlier, make it possible for the individual to realise the conditioned state in which he is, and thereby to attain the Unconditioned. Considering the requirements of the path, the Way to *Nirvāṇa* is described as the culmination of a person's moral development (*sīla*), intuitional or spiritual development (*samādhi*), as well as his intellectual or cognitive development (*paññā*). The Buddha was once asked "whether he hoped to save one-third of the world, one-half of the world or the whole world by offering this Way of Salvation", to which he replied that he did not claim to save one-third of humanity, but that just as a skilful doorkeeper guarding the only entrance to the palace knows that all those who seek the haven of this palace must enter by this door, even so he knew that all those who in the past were saved, who in the present are being saved and who in future will be saved, have entered, are entering and will enter by this door.

Such is the teaching of Early Buddhism which is offered as a self-consistent scientific hypothesis touching matters of religion and morality which each person can verify for himself. Not being based on revelation, the fact that it has been verified by the Buddha and hundreds of his disciples and is capable of being verified by every earnest seeker, is put forward as the criterion of its truth. The empirical and pragmatic test of science is, for the Buddha, the test of true religion. The faith that he requires is the trust that is required to put to test a certain philosophy of life by devoting one's entire being to living it every moment of one's life. And its worth is to be realised by its fruits by each person for himself. Like the scientists working in other fields, the Buddhas or the Perfect Ones have merely discovered these truths which are there for all time. The Buddhas have preached them for the good of the world. Each one has to seek and work out his own salvation; no one can save another and the Perfect Ones do merely point the way.

It would be seen that such a religion is in accord with the temper and findings of science. As such, Buddhism is not likely to be at variance with science so long as scientists confine themselves to their methodology and their respective fields without making a dogma of materialism.

As for any purpose, the Buddhist view is that the world as such has no purpose to accomplish, though individuals in it may choose their own ends and thus make their lives purposeful; the end recommended by Buddhism being *Nirvāṇa*. The Buddha would argue that if the world had a purpose to be attained in a final consummation, then either salvation would be assured for all or some would be foredoomed and damned for eternity; but according to the Buddha there is no necessity or inevitability in progress; no one is destined to attain Nirvāṇa unless he wishes to. As for moral values, Buddhism upholds their objectivity, for according to the Law of Karma, a drunkard, for instance, unless he repents (i.e. changes his ways) tends to be reborn as a moron whatever the opinions or wishes of the drunkard or the members of his society may be.

THE RELATION OF BUDDHISM TO MODERN SCIENCE

by

ROBERT F. SPENCER

There can be no question that Buddhism is the one system, excepting perhaps science itself, which achieves an objective and detached view about the nature and destiny of man. This striking objectivity divorces the Buddhist system from the realm of religion and allies it at once with the kind of scientific search for truth which characterized India in the Gupta and other early periods of its civilization and which affords a major pre-occupation to most of the intellectual world—both East and West—of today. Buddhism, this writer contends, is not properly a religion; it is a system for life and living in a world which is circumscribed with difficulty and beset with suffering. Buddhism is not a religion, if, in scientific terms, we define religion as a mystic experience, a psychic thrill. It is not a religion because it de-emphasizes faith in the unknown and unknowable and it rejects dogmatism. However much these latter features may obtrude themselves in Buddhist lands, no serious student can regard them as other than superfluous growths, digressions from the scientifically conceived Dharma of the Founder. This paper holds that in the strictest sense, Buddhism as a system is comparable to a scientific endeavour.

But there is also a difference: the Buddhist thinker is clear as to his aims; if he uses science and its methods, he does so with the realization that science is a means to an end and not an end in itself. In other words, the Buddhist sees in science reflections of principles expressed and reiterated by Lord Buddha at a time when there was no absolute methodology of science as such. Since today the world is wedded to the methods of science, we have only to note how wholly compatible with science is the system founded in India about 2,500 years ago. Modern scientific achievement serves merely to lend added perspective to the concepts of impermanence, of the illusory quality, and of *anātman* which were put forth so long ago. As an end in itself, science may solve immediate problems; it feeds more people so that there are more people to feed; it prolongs life and finds more effective means of destroying life. Science, as viewed today, is nothing more than a method and to make a cult of it, to find in it the answer to problems and questions of the ultimate forms of human destiny, is rank error. It is making a dogma of science where no religious emotion or attitude are ever intended. This indeed was the fallacy of some of the sectarian forms of ancient Hinduism; in seeking to explain the universe by means of an atomic theory, however correctly conceived, the Brahmins of India of the past stopped dead and found human salvation, if such it may be called, in science and scientific activity. Nor is the contemporary world too different despite the fact that the scientific goal is material rather than spiritual.

The method of science admits primarily the formulation of an hypothesis, the testing of that hypothesis, and the stating of a new hypothesis on the basis of knowledge obtained by such experimentation. Lord Buddha experimented with ideas, not with things—he employed the crucible of life in which to measure human experience and he came up with a detached and tested answer.

Science is characterized by its "tough-mindedness". The search for truth is not always easy, nor indeed, always pleasant. It has been said that the truth may hurt. It does, but it remains truth for all that. Pristine Buddhism offers an attempt, a successful one, it may be added, to come to grips with truth in an objective way. To those of us who, now living, are seeking a few moments of respite, of relief from worry, in short, of what might be called happiness, the Buddha says in effect: "All right, just remember, it doesn't last; it may be here today but it is never permanent". Just as science seeks to define its answers objectively, without emotion, so also does Buddhism hit squarely at the target and, free from emotional stress, informs us concisely what is what. We may not like it and we may have to toughen ourselves to take it, but it is proven to be.

An example of the kind of scientific "tough-mindedness" which the Buddhist has to develop is seen in the concept of *karma*. What indeed could be simpler and yet what could be more scientifically conceived? If one chooses, one may take on faith, to be sure, the *saṃsāra* principle. Objectively, however, previous existences, however envisioned in time or space, remain a matter of complete indifference. What is significant is that "I" am not the same individual that "I" was yesterday, an year ago, or even a moment ago. The ego has changed, the physical form has changed, however imperceptibly. Moreover, the "I" of the individual, having volition and free will, can and does act. Acts, however, are pre-conditioned by foregoing acts. A deed of today begets its effects tomorrow, effects on future action and thought. In the view of this writer, this is the karmic principle with meaning and application. It is scientific; there is nothing esoteric about it.

So much has been said regarding the relationship between Buddhism and the natural sciences, that it is scarcely worth belaboring the point further here. The nature of matter, the nature of physical reality, problems of space and time are all implicit in Buddhist teachings. This writer must confess that he cannot care less about such mystical relationships as are conceived between mind and matter. His interests lie in the connections between Buddhism and the social sciences, that wide area which seeks to understand the relation between man and man, not that between atom and an unpopulated universe.

In such of the social sciences as anthropology and sociology, an attempt is made to understand how men behave in groups and why they act as they do. A related aspect is seen in economics and in its handmaiden, political science. Still further, may be added the discipline which seeks to evaluate the individual, psychology. In all of these fields, one thought becomes paramount: human beings act because of their conditioning—the anthropologist would say because of their cultural heritage. We come to realize that what one people regards as right, another may view as wholly wrong. The social sciences teach us the relativism of human behaviour.

Granted that human behaviour be relative, it follows that there are no absolute concepts of good or evil. Indeed, good and evil are wholly relative. As a trained social scientist, one who has information regarding the differing ways of the peoples of the world, the writer accepts this. However, only in Buddhism is some order restored from the resulting chaos. Note that the Buddha does not say—"Thou shalt not....". He does say that it is a good idea to avoid certain kinds of behaviour and he issues a series of wholly positive injunctions on his followers. Regardless of background, regardless of belief, regardless of economic or political systems, Buddhism has application. It makes sense as nothing else can to restore balance to men. Not that it is even desirable to effect a balance from the Buddhist point of view. To realise the concept of *anicca* is unquestionably for all men enough.

But the Buddhist could assist his own goals by a realisation of the objectivity of the social scientist. Here the scientist takes a view of detachment toward his fellow man. He does not seek amelioration. The Buddhist can and should do the same; by so doing, he may achieve by indirection solutions to the problem of human suffering. Lord Buddha realised that the man who helped himself would inevitably help others. He comes concretely to grips with problems of society and personality. Psycho-analysis may in some measure be compared with enlightenment but the enlightened man does not need to be told how to live with his fellows. The nature of enlightenment brings this inevitably about. The Buddhist can adopt the contemplative detachment of a scientist. In so doing, he makes himself a better Buddhist and follows infinitely more closely the basic precepts. Objectivity in human affairs remains his watchword.

ANICCAM—THE BUDDHIST THEORY OF IMPERMANENCE

An Approach from the Standpoint of Modern Science and Philosophy

by

BHIKKHU NANAJIVAKO

> —Is the eye...the shape...
> visual consciousness, permanent or impermanent?
> —Impermanent, reverend sir.
> —But is what is impermanent, anguish or happiness?
> —Anguish, reverend sir.
> —Is it right to regard that which is impermanent
> anguish, and liable to alteration as
> "This is mine, this am I, this is my self"?
> —No, reverend sir.[1]

Insights and discoveries revealed to human minds about 2500 years ago, at the time of the Buddha (or even several centuries before that time), may have caused deep and revolutionary effects in the evolution of existing world-views, no less important than the discoveries of Galileo and Copernicus have been for the eventual collapse of the world-view of medieval Christian civilization. These latter discoveries, which mark the onset of modern civilization, have become so much a part of commonplace or general information that they can be imparted to children in the lowest grades of elementary education, and are normally absorbed by them without difficulty.

The idea of impermanence and of a ceaseless change, due to the never-ending "chain" of causes and effects (the subject which we are attempting to approach in its Buddhist version of *aniccam*) has, in its broad meaning, become one of our stereotyped and oversimplified truisms, reduced, both in its formal and substantial significance, to a mere rudiment of conventional word-meaning. As such, it may still have impressed us at the level of nursery rhymes and even of some grammar-school classics in the history of literature. (If I had to choose a deeper adequation founded on a modern poet's more complex philosophical intuition, I would not hesitate to select the lines from T. S. Eliot's Quartets:

> Ash on an old man's sleeve
> Is all the ash the burnt roses leave
> ....
> Water and fire succeed
> The town, the pasture and the weed.)

We might hope to rediscover the original significance and historical purport of such truisms only if we were to look for them purposively, guided by some subjective impressions of individual or particular cases, and by the consequences of their concrete application in actual scientific or philosophical theories. This is what I am about to hint at with the help of a few examples.

One: As a young teacher, when for the first time I tried to explain to children of about twelve years of age the biological process of growing cabbages and potatoes, my emphasis on the importance of dung (I did not use the technical term "fertilizer") happened to be so impressive that the next day a mother came to complain against my "direct method" and "drastic naturalism" in visual teaching. Her child had been so affected by my discourse as to develop an acute loathing against food. Thus I was impressed how easily our most commonplace truisms about the laws of nature—whose discovery, once upon a time, may have been treated (and even punished) as revolutionary by respectable and authoritative social instructions—can still reveal themselves unexpectedly in their full overpowering force to the fresh and innocent minds of new generations.

Two: In my own generation of teenagers, between the two wars in Europe, the deadlock between science and religion was so complete that secondary school curricula were bound to provoke in our minds an unavoidable crisis of conscience. Teachers on the whole were totally involved in this struggle of convictions, keen to win us over to one side or the other.

The side of science against religion was normally the stronger one. Since that time religion, defeated in Europe, has become more and more of a prohibited fruit, and has therefore acquired a new attractive force for juvenile minds. This is true not only in the eastern parts of Europe, since science is far from being a privilege of communism. An anti-scientific tendency in European ("continental") philosophy has even become predominant, on account of the moral catastrophe which still preoccupies the minds of our generation more than any other problem concerning "man's position in the universe".

The central issue in this conflict between science and religion, at least from our youthful bias at that time, was of course the problem of *anattā* ("no-soul"), to express it by the corresponding Buddhist term. Laws governing *Processes* of causes and effects were, however, scientifically explained—or at least were so understood by our unripe minds, under the impression of the open dispute between science and (Christian) religion. The explanations were not yet in terms of a scientific equivalent to a pure *anicca-vādo* (theory of impermanence), which would imply a denial of the underlying material substantiality of the world. Instead of that, explanations given to us at that time still followed the classical Greek pattern of mechanistic materialism or static atomism, which was the closest to the Buddhist understanding of the *uccheda-vādo* (theory of destruction), whose believers are described in Pāli texts in the following terms:

> ...He then hears the Perfect one expounding the teaching for the removal of all grounds for "views," of all prejudices, obsessions, dogmas and biases, for the stilling of all processes, for the relinquishment of all substrata of existence, for the extirpation of craving, for dispassion, cessation, extinction. He then thinks, "I shall be annihilated, I shall be destroyed ! No longer shall I exist !" Hence he grieves, is depressed and laments; beating his breast, he weeps, and dejection befalls him. Thus, bhikkhus, is there anxiety about realities. (M.22)

To this, the only authentic answer is:

> Since in this very life a *tathāgata* (in this case, generally understood as a human being in the widest sense) is not to

> be regarded as existing in truth, in reality, is it proper for you to assert: 'As I understand the doctrine taught by the Exalted One, insofar as a bhikkhu has destroyed the *āsavas* (life's "intoxicants" or passions) he is broken up and perishes when body is broken up, he exists not after death'? (S. XXII, 85, 33)

The logical possibility of such an answer is excluded by the premise itself. The same premise, however, excludes also the opposite, affirmative, possibility. (We shall return to this problem, as understood by contemporary philosophy, in section Five.)

It is important to underline here that, on the same premise, *uccheda-vādo*, or simply the *materialistic belief* in a substantial "destruction" of any form of being, is the extreme opposite of any authentic *nihilism* in ontology and epistemology (theory of being and theory of knowledge). Only an explicitly idealistic philosophy, "looking upon the world as a bubble, as a mirage," (Dph. 170) can be nihilistic in some respect, while *uccheda-vādo* as a "theory of destruction" necessarily presupposes an existentially rooted belief in material substance.

It was just in this sense, in the midst of the battleground between science and religion, and on the eve of a world war, that the children of the first half of the 20th century had to face the fatality of a physical and moral destruction, scientifically and infallibly precalculated, as experience was about to prove. Yet, just over the edge of our intellectual horizon was dawning a time, for science at least, of acquiring a completely different position vis a vis the problem of impermanence and relativity as affecting the deepest subatomic structure of the world—a position considerably closer to the Buddhist idea of *aniccam*.

Three: Since 1927, Bertrand Russell's book, *An Outline of Philosophy*, has been widely quoted as one of the best popular presentations of the radical change in the scientific world-view stemming from Einstein's theory of relativity and of the resulting development of nuclear physics. I shall try to elicit from Russell's statements, as far as the present draft of pointers to our essential problem may permit, the rejection of the *substance-view* by modern science, because it is this rejection that constitutes the core of the Buddhist *anicca-vādo* as a foundation (at least in the *ti-lakkhaṇam* scheme) of both ***dukkham and anattā.***

To start with, let us define the idea of physical "substance" by means of its basic description and philosophical implication as stated in the *Sutta-piṭakam* sources. The problem of substance, as defined by scientific (*lokāyatam*) theories at the time of the Buddha, finds its classical formulation, categorical delimitation and solution in concise terms in his concluding answer to Kevaddoho (D.11):

> —Where do earth, water, fire and wind; long and short; fine and coarse; pure and impure, no footing find ? Where is it that both name and form die out, leaving no trace behind ?
> —When intellection (*viññāṇam*) ceases they all cease too.

For the categorical relation of mind and matter (or "name and form," *nāma-rūpam*, as implied in the foregoing formulation), the following statement of the Buddha is the most adequate and also the best-known in connection with our subject:

> It would be better, bhikkhus, for the unlearned worldling to regard this body, built up of the four elements, as his self rather than the mind. For it is evident that this body may last for a year, for two years, for three, four or ten years... or even for a hundred years and more. But that which is called thought, or mind, or consciousness, continuously, during day and night, arises as one thing, and passes away as another thing (S.12,62).

Now, let us give a few quotations from Bertrand Russell.[2] First, as regards substance-matter, he says:

> In former days, you could believe it on a philosophical ground that the soul is a substance and all substances are indestructible....But the notion of substance, in the sense of a permanent entity with changing states, is no longer applicable to the world.
>
> A wave in the sea persists for a longer or shorter time: the waves that I see dashing themselves to pieces on the Cornish coast may have come all the way from Brazil, but that does not mean that a "thing" has travelled across the

Atlantic; it means only that a certain *process of change* has travelled.

(Einstein's theory of relativity) has philosophical consequences which are, if possible, even more important. The substitution of space-time for space and time has made the category of substance less applicable than formerly, since the essence of substance was persistence through time, and there is now no one cosmic time.

We found that matter, in modern science, has lost its solidity and substantiality; it has become a mere ghost haunting the scenes of its former splendour....The notion of matter, in modern physics, has become absorbed into the notion of energy.

We cannot say that "matter is the cause of our sensations." ....In a word, "matter" has become no more than a conventional shorthand for stating *causal laws concerning events.*

Thus we are committed to causation as an *a priori* belief without which we should have no reason for supposing that there is a "real" chair (or any *thing*) at all.

Next, as regards the *theory of events*, we note that the idea of fixed and static elements of 'matter' has been replaced by that of undeterminable 'events' corresponding to the quantum electrodynamic field theory in nuclear physics, which comes very close to the conception of a non-physical but purely phenomenological idea of *dhamma,* implied in its primitive significance by *khaṇika-vādo*, a theory of momentariness, of the *Abhidhamma-piṭakam.* (This latter aspect, explicitly philosophical, will be sketched in *Five*, below.) Of this Russell writes:

Everything in the world is composed of "events."...An "event" is something occupying a small finite amount of space-time....Events are not impenetrable, as matter is supposed to be; on the contrary, every event in space-time is overlapped by other events.

I assume that every event is contemporaneous with events that are not contemporaneous with each other; this is what is meant by saying that every event lasts for a finite time.... Time is wholly relational.

Space-time order, as well as space-time points, result from the relations between events.

Compare with this last statement, and with those that follow, the assertion of Buddhaghosa in *Aṭṭhasālini*: "By time the sage described the mind, and by mind described the time."

Lastly, Russell says of *mental events*:

> An important group of events, namely percepts, may be called "mental".
>
> Mentality is an affair of causal laws, not of the quality of single events, and also, mentality is a matter of degree.
>
> What is mind ?...Mind must be a group of mental events, since we have rejected the view that it is a single entity such as the *ego* was formerly supposed to be....Its constitution corresponds however to "the unity of one 'experience'."

As a result of these considerations, Russell concludes that "first of all, you must cut out the word 'I': the person who believes is an inference, not a part of what you know immediately."

Finally, the logical possibility of an *uccheda-vādo* (theory o destruction) "heresy" is explicitly eliminated even on this level of merely scientific considerations: "Is a mind a structure of material units ? I think it is clear that the answer to this question is in the negative."

We can conclude this survey by accepting without any further reserve Russell's statement: "The problems we have been raising are none of them new, but they suffice to show that our everyday views of the world and of our relations to it are unsatisfactory."

Four: Recently, field theory, as a replacement for the abandoned substance theory in physics, has found increasing application—at least as an hypothetical analogy—in other spheres of scientific thought, and even more in philosophical speculations limited to possible (and sometimes to impossible) extensions of "special sciences". Its application to parapsychology is of particular interest for the extension of the subject in which we are interested beyond the strictly physical sphere of being.

It is Gardner Murphy who has given us the most logical and exclusive elaboration of a parapsychological analogy of field theory, as far as I know. A summarized recapitulation of his thesis is as follows:

The action of living matter on living matter is never a case of single cell acting only on single cell. The structural whole or field is always involved. The field principle may hold in psychics as well as in physics, and a psychic field may extend backwards and forwards in time as well as onwards in space. The question, "Does personality survive death?" is therefore, in Murphy's view, not a reasonable question to ask. If any psychical *activity* survives, it will become an aspect of different fields and will thus take on new qualities and new structural relationships. It is evident that for him "all personal activities are constantly changing context and interacting with those of others, and it may be that each one becomes part of the cosmic process."[3]

Another worker in the field of parapsychology, C. D. Broad, investigating *The Mind and its Place in Nature* from the standpoint of a possible "survival" of the "*psi* component," draws the conclusion, from the same basic analogy with physics, that "we need no longer suppose that, although a surviving *psi* component may be bodiless, it is necessarily unextended and unlocalized, for we are nowadays well accustomed to such phenomena as electro-magnetic fields which cannot be called bodies in the ordinary sense but which still have structure and definite properties and dispositions. We must not think of it (i.e. of the surviving *psi*-component) as something on which an experience makes an impression as a seal does on a ball of wax. On the contrary, such a substanceless theory implies a greater degree of survival than the mere persistence of an inactive *psi* component."[4]

Exponents of the same parapsychological theory also maintain that their hypothesis might offer a more adequate basis for explanation of subconscious phenomena investigated by psychoanalysis, particularly Jung's archetypes, than the initial Freudian attempts, which have been characterized since the first as a scientifically untenable Platonic analogy with "pigeon holes" as the basic structure of the soul.

All these more or less *ad hoc* analogies with the field theory in physics can be brought down as well to an earlier metaphysical hypothesis, formulated on a broader philosophical basis already by William James, in his *Pluralistic Universe* (1909).[5] Speaking of the structure of "our inner life", James says:

> Every bit of us at every moment is part and parcel of a wider self....May not you and I be confluent in a higher consciousness, and confluently active there, though we now know it not ?...The analogies with...facts of psychical research, so called, and with those of religious experience, establish...a decidedly formidable probability in favour (of the following pluralistic hypothesis:)
>
> Why should we envelop our many with the 'one' that brings so many poison in its train ?... (instead of accepting) along with the superhuman consciousness the notion that it is not all-embracing; the notion, in other words, that there is a God, but that he is finite, either in power or in knowledge, or in both at once.

This is exactly the basic distinction between the Vedāntic and the Buddhist conception of God, or gods, implying also the reason why James, in some respects, was in favour of a polytheistic conception, as a "result of our criticism of the absolute", in the same context.

Five: Such adaptation of hypotheses borrowed *ad hoc* from heterogeneous fields of science could and should be ultimately verified and explained only by proper philosophical investigation, using autonomous methods and established on its own, purely anthropological ground. Since the beginning of the 20th century this has indeed been done, always more clearly and explicitly. The results have been considerable, at least as far as the problem of our primordial concern is involved: the human value aspect of *aniccam*, its fundamental significance in connection with both *dukkham* and *anattā*.

The proper philosophical attitude was defined, not as pertaining to the physical but rather to the *historical* world-view, as early as the end of the 19th century, by Wilhelm Dilthey, founder of the modern philosophy of culture:

> The final pronouncement of the historical world-view is that human accomplishment of every sort is relative, that *everything is moving in process and nothing is stable.*

And yet this historical orientation has not maintained a position of predominant importance in 20th century European philosophy. The most prominent philosopher of culture in the middle of this century, Karl Jaspers, in discussing the priority of the question "What is man?" (as formulated by Kant) points out that this priority "does not mean that the knowledge of being is to be replaced by the knowledge of man. Being still remains the essential, but man can approach it only through his existence as a man", i.e., through his historicity.[6]

Following Edmund Husserl, who established the most widely adopted logical and epistemological platform for European or continental philosophy in this century, the problem of *being* has acquired and sustained a role of central importance. In order to avoid its gross misunderstanding, it is necessary, especially from our Buddhist standpoint, to note that Husserl's basic postulate, "Back to the things themselves", does not in any way imply a substantialist meaning of "things" in the classical, physically oriented ontology or theory of being, which has been rejected by modern physics. The significance of "being" has radically changed with the achievement of a deeper insight into both its physical and historical structure. This is revealed very clearly in the analysis of being by Nicolai Hartmann who, more than Husserl and his closer followers, concentrated on implications of the ontological problem in the natural sciences.

In this respect, the standpoint of A. N. Whitehead in Anglo-American philosophy comes closest to that of N. Hartmann. Russell's theory of infinitesimal "space-time events" was not much more than an attempt to reduce to a pale rationalized scheme Whitehead's metaphysical conception of "actual occasions" and "throbbing actualities", understood as "pulsation of experience" whose "drops" or "puffs of existence" guided by an internal teleology in their "concrescence" (analogous to the Buddhist *saṅkhāra* in karmic formations) join the "stream of existence" (*bhavaṅga-soto*).

The core of the *abhidhammo* conception of the "stream of existence" consists in its "theory of momentariness" *khaṇikavādo*. Its modern analogy has found its first and best formulation in plain terms in the philosophy of William James, especially in his essay *Does Consciousness Exist?*, where the "stream of consciousness" or "stream of thinking" (which, "when scrutinized, reveals itself to consist chiefly of the stream of my breathing") is elicited from his basic theory of "pure experience", defined as "the instant field of the present...this succession of an emptiness and fullness that have reference to each other and are of one flesh"—

succession "in small enough pulses", which "is the essence of the phenomenon". In the same connection, as "the result of our criticism of the absolute", the metaphysical and metapsychical idea of a "central self" is reduced by James to "the conscious self of the moment".[7] The well-known Buddhist thesis of "no-self" (*anattā*), or of a soul-less psychology, is based on the same "theory of momentariness".

This is also one of the points—and the most significant one—on which the philosophical conception of James coincides with Bergson. Terminologically at least, in Bergson's designation of the same "stream" as "*flux du vecu*", the word "vecu" ("lived") seems to come closest to the meaning of the Pāli *bhavaṅgo*, suggesting the "articulated" (*-aṅgo*) texture of life-experience.

In Husserl's interpretation, "things" are simply taken to mean "whatever is given", that which we "see" in consciousness, and this "given" is called phenomenal in the sense that it "appears" to our consciousness. The Greek word "phenomenon" does not necessarily indicate that there is an unknown thing behind phenomena (as in Kant's philosophy or in the Vedānta), or a "back-stage" being, as Nietzsche ironically exposed it. From our standpoint, it is important to emphasize that Husserl's phenomenological method "is neither deductive nor empirical, but consists in *pointing* to what is given and *elucidating* it".[8] It claims, in other words, to be *yathā-bhūtam*, or "adequate to (actual) being."

The analysis of the original meaning of the Greek term "phenomenon" has been performed in masterly fashion by Martin Heidegger.[9] The word phenomenon (from the verb *phainesthal*, "let see", which is similar to the Pāli *ehi-passiko*) has two meanings relevant for philosophy. The first is "to show itself", the second, "to seem as". Contemporary phenomenological philosophy uses it in the first sense, as "merely letting something be seen, letting entities be perceived". The second meaning, indicating something which seems to "remain hidden, or which relapses or gets covered again, or shows itself only 'in disguise' ", points to the *historical process* of constructing theories and "views" (Greek *doxa*, Sanskrit *dṛṣṭi*, Pāli *diṭṭhi*) by which the primordially "uncovered" phenomena are rather concealed again, or kept in disguise.

The same basic idea is adopted by Nicolai Hartmann: "That a being is 'in-itself' means to say that it exists actually and not only for us.... Being-in-itself does not need to be proved, it is given as the world itself is given."[10] Hartmann's most valuable contribution, however, is his entrance into the profound analysis of what was called above the second meaning of the philosophical term 'phenomenon'. His analysis distinguishes "spheres" and "levels" of being: Broadly, there are two primary spheres, designated as real and ideal being. In the sphere of the real, four structural levels are distinguished: matter, life, consciousness and mind.

In contexts eliciting such statements, it appears more and more obvious, from the Buddhist standpoint, how closely the meaning of the term phenomenon, as used in contemporary philosophy, approximates the basic meaning of *dhamma* in the *abhidhamma* theory. (The last instance quoted from Hartmann may remind us even more specifically of the *khandha structures.*)

However, beyond the possibility of extending this analogy of phenomenon as disclosure of "being-in-itself" understood as a process, it is felt more and more by several contemporary European philosophers (just as was the case in the original Buddhist counterpart) that the ontological purport of being, thus understood as phenomenon or *dhammo*, must still be limited by a critical principle of essentially deeper significance. This principle has found its first—and until now its clearest—logical formulation in the *catu-koṭikam* (tetralemma) rule by the Buddha, as he regularly applies it to the *avyaktāni* or "not designated" problems, or "dialectical antinomies"[11] of speculative thought: "Neither being, nor non-being, nor both being-and-non-being, nor neither-being-nor-non-being" can express the existential purport and content of human reality. The word "being", or any other derivative from the verb "to be", cannot adequately express the immediate intuition (*vipassanā*) of existence, or the essence of actuality (as *paramāttho*).

This deficiency of the basic ontological term "being" has been subtly analyzed by Heidegger in his *Introduction to Metaphysics*. Yet, with him, the philosophy of existence (or human actuality) has taken a prevalently ontological direction (as a phenomenological analysis of being). It has become a philosophy of our human being-in-the-world, and consequently a philosophy of "anguish" or *dukkham*, even though it was soon felt that this ontological turning does not, and cannot, adequately reflect either the primordial motives or the ultimate scope of existential thinking. Without entering into the historical background of such inner divergences in contemporary philosophy, I should like to point out a few symptomatic objections which can be compared in their radically anti-ontological attitude with the principle of the Buddha as formulated above.

According to the Buddha, the person reaping the fruits of good and bad actions (in a future life) is neither the same one who has committed these actions nor a different one. The same principle applies to the structural identification of a person in any other respect and circumstance, in the stream of one single physical life.

The French philosopher Gabriel Marcel, discussing the problem of the structural unity of human personality, comes (at least at the basic level) to the conclusion that "the relation between my body and myself cannot be described as either 'being' or 'having': I *am* my body and yet I cannot identify myself with it."[12] "Existing" does not mean being an object. On this supposition, Marcel develops his critical analysis of the two inadequate extreme terms of existence in his main work, *Being and Having*.

Another representative of the same trend in French philosophy, Jean Wahl, seems to approximate more nearly the actual meaning of the Buddha's *avyaktāni* (specified above), not from formal logical or even linguistic considerations, but rather out of an essentially congenial understanding of the deeper problem: "We are concerned with questions which, strictly speaking, belong to solitary meditation and cannot be subjects of discourse."[13]

Nicolas Berdyaev, an explicitly religious philosopher close to the same group, has given one of the clearest formulations of the point under discussion:

"The problem which faces us is: Is *being* a product of objectification? Is not the concept of being concerned with being *qua* concept, does being possess existence at all?...Why is ontology impossible? Because it is always a knowledge of objectifying existence. In an ontology the idea of being is objectified and an objectification is already an existence which is alienated in the objectification. So that in ontology—in every ontology—existence vanishes....It is only in subjectivity that one may know existence, not in objectivity. In my opinion, the central idea has vanished in the ontology of Heidegger and Sartre."[14]

In agreement with Dilthey's principle, quoted above, establishing the historical world-view of the cultural sciences independently from the scientific investigation of essentially objective physical nature, Heidegger has limited his inquiry on "time as the horizon for all understanding of being". Against that background, he has criticized and abandoned the old substantialist ontology. For him, "temporality is the very being of human reality". The relation time-mind, as quoted above from Buddhaghosa's *Aṭṭhasālinī*, is for Heidegger also, exhaustive for both terms. And yet Berdyaev, like the other anti-ontologist philosophers mentioned here, criticizes even this essential turning in contemporary "anthropological ontology", as at least a partial failure to understand authentic existential experience: "As a man Heidegger is deeply troubled by this world of care, fear, death and daily dullness". Despite this, and beyond that sincerity, his philosophy "is not existential philosophy, and the depth of existence does not make itself felt in it".[15]

The reason for this was stated clearly and explicitly by Karl Jaspers, who was the first to criticize and abandon the ontological position in contemporary European philosophy, at the same time that Heidegger undertook his essential reform of its fundamental conception. In the view of Jaspers, "the ideal followed by ontologies is the perfectioning of the rational structure of the objectified world. Technical sciences have to help us bring about engineered existences." Jaspers was, from the very beginning of his philosophical *critique* (about 1930), extremely aware of the danger of such scientific technicalization of human existence: "As an attempt to bind us to objectified being, ontology sublates freedom." In his view, it is only "as potential existence that I am able to lift myself up from bondage. My chains will thus become the material of being. . . ." The opposite way of an "engineered" civilization will transform me into a slave of that "material" and this actually is the typical form of suffering, of *dukkham*, by which "man in the modern age" is oppressed.[16]

In his advanced years, Jaspers has discovered the Buddhist philosopher Nāgārjuna as one of the most congenial minds,[17] while Heidegger, when reading D.T. Suzuki's *Essays on Zen*

Buddhism, confessed that this was exactly what he had tried to express all his life long.

Six: It was doubt of the material substance of the world which, to a considerable extent, provoked the problem of verifying the very idea of being, of the "selfhood" of the world, both in its exterior aspect and in that which is interior to the human being-in-the-world. What "doubt" was at the outset of critical philosophy in the period of its substantialist and objectifying orientation (following Descartes), *disappointment*, the "unsatisfactoriness" of the world, has become for the actual, subjectively oriented or introverted, humanistic philosophy of existence.

One of the best expressions of this turning can be found in some of the statements of Gabriel Marcel, who, by the way, defines his religious philosophy as a "doctrine of hope". Its basic postulate is that philosophy must be "transobjective, personal, dramatic, indeed tragic. 'I am not witnessing a spectacle'; we should remind ourselves of this everyday".[18] The Buddhist implication of this basic attitude may be pursued still further in the earlier formulation by Kierkegaard: "Life is a masquerade....Your occupation consists in preserving your hiding place....In fact you are nothing; *you are merely a relation to others*, and what you are, you are by virtue of this relation....When the enchantment of illusion is broken, when existence begins to totter, then too does despair manifest itself as that which was at the bottom. Despair itself is a negativity, unconsciousness of it is a new negativity.... This is the sickness unto death".[19]

It is only by abandoning the attitude of fascination for the "spectacle" of the statically staged "Being" of the world that man becomes sufficiently movable, that he is fit to plunge into the stream of existence, no longer attached to some stage-prop or "remainder". It is only then that he can really start swimming along that stream of *saṃsāro*, realizing that it is pure and simple *aniccam* or impermanent flux, and that he can eventually become aware of the advantage of "crossing" it.

This is the point which contemporary European philosophy seems to be about to realize. It is essential for this realization that the principles of *aniccam* and *dukkham* be inseparably reconnected through the intuition of their immediate interaction. In the actual situation, it will no longer even be necessary to deduce explicitly the idea of *anattā* as the dynamic resultant of the confrontation of the first two principles. Just like *aniccam*, *anattā* has already become a truism for most Europeans, whom a standardized mental training, both scientific and philosophical, has carried beyond the God and Soul dogma.[20] The phantom of the Western version of a materialistic *uccheda-vādo* is likewise about to be dispelled. The critical missing link has only been between impermanence (*aniccam*) and suffering (*dukkham*). Due to the objectifying nature of scientific thinking, this link could never be revealed by a philosophy of nature subservient to science, not even of the type of Russell's popular literary criticism quoted above. It is obvious that only an existential experience of *dukkham*, suffering or "anguish", could bring about this realization.

Today we have to thank, for this realization, the catastrophic results and further consequences, still being suffered, of two world wars in the 20th century. That is why a new philosophy, already nascent on the eve of the second world war, has emerged in Europe explicitly as a philosophy of *conscience*, rather than of mere *consciousness*. It should appear equally obvious that in such a philosophy there is no longer any place for the stubborn false dilemma: philosophy *or* religion. This last problem, which concerns "philosophical faith", is more important for Buddhism than for any other religion. It has found its best diagnostical expression in several essays of Karl Jaspers, from which we extract a few hints:

> It is questionable whether *faith* is possible *without religion*. Philosophy originates in this question. . . .Man deprived of his faith by the loss of his religion is devoting more decisive thought to the nature of his own being. . . .No longer does the revealed Deity upon whom all is dependent come first, and no longer the world that exists around us; what comes first is man, who, however, cannot make terms with himself as being, but strives to transcend himself. . . .The unsheltered individual gives our epoch its physiognomy. . . . (Formerly) the authority of a church sheltered him and sustained him, gave him peace and happiness. . . .Today philosophy is the only refuge for those who, in full awareness, are not sheltered by religion.[21]

Obviously, "faith" is here no longer understood as a belief in any revelation, but as reasonable trust in a qualified spiritual guide whose moral and intellectual capacities have to be carefully tested in each single case by a sound and mature criterion (*apannako dhammo*) such as was established by the Buddha in his critical discourses on religion, *Apannaka-suttam* and *Canki-suttam* (M. 60 and 95), in order to exclude empty and blind transmission of religious traditions "as a basket handed over from one to the other", or in "a string of blind men". "One oneself is the guardian of oneself; what other guardian could there be?" (Dph 160)

Jean-Paul Sartre is another philosopher who, though himself not religious, realizes the tremendous importance of the religious problem from the bias of our critical age, and still more specifically from the bias of the deepest metaphysical implications of the idea of *aniccam*, as non-substantiality, undermining the scientific foundation of 19th century materialism: The tragic situation of human reality in the world consists in the fact, that due to his karmic "freedom", man "is not what he is, man is what he is not". This statement, whose implications have scandalized many conservative Christian minds, nevertheless corresponds to the gist of St. Augustine's thought as rendered by Jaspers out of a different deeply religious concern with the undeniable facticity of the same existential situation: "I am myself, but I can fail myself. I must put my trust in myself, but I cannot rely on myself".[22]

As for Sartre, his first deduction from this basic realization of *anicca-anattā* is that as such "man is a useless passion". "Human reality is the pure effort to become God without there being any given substratum for that effort.... Desire expresses this endeavor....Fundamentally man *is the desire to be*." As such, he is always only a "project"—ceaselessly "catapulted" from the past to the future (as Ortegay Gasset has formulated it), without a natural possibility of finding poise in his own present. This is the tragedy of his "temporalization", whose ultimate meaning is *aniccam*. This is how "the existence of desire as a human fact is sufficient to prove that human reality is a lack". How, then, is a possibility of ultimate escape or "liberation" conceivable? It is because human reality "is a being such that in its being, its being is in question in the form of a project of being". On this basis only, "We can ascertain more exactly what is the being of the self: it is value".[23]

He who wants to delve deeper into such possibilities, it would seem, should follow the advice of Gabriel Marcel, or of Berdyaev, and try to cross beyond the possibilities expressed in any philosophy of being. The Buddhist fitting, or "raft", though considerably larger in its basic frame, is readily adaptable to their explicit requirements: "Neither being, nor non-being, nor both being-and-non-being, nor neither-being-nor-non-being".

NOTES

[1]*Majjhima-nikāyo*, discourse 146, and several other texts. Quotations from Pali *suttas* are adapted mainly from the Pali Text Society's editions of the Translation Series. References in the text are to the *Majjhimanikāyo* (M), *Dīgha-nikāyo* (D), *Saṃyutta-nikāyo* (S), Dhammapadam (D).

[2]Quotations from *An Outline of Philosophy*, 3rd impression. London, Allen and Unwin, 1941, pp. 309, 290, 304, 294, 290, 5, 287, 288, 289, 291, 292, 296, 297, 11, 300, 14.

[3]Quoted according to R. Heywood, *The Sixth Sense, an Inquiry into Extra-Sensory Perception*, London, Pan Books, 1959, pp. 205-210.

[4]See also his book, *Religion, Philosophy and Psychical Research*, London, Routledge and Kegan Paul, 1953, and R. Heywood, op. cit., pp. 219-222.

[5]The following quotations are from *Classic American Philosophers*, General Editor M. H. Fisch, New York, Applenton-Century-Crofts, 1951, pp. 163, 164.

[6]K. Jaspers, *The Great Philosophers*, ed. by R. Hart-Davis, London, 1962, p. 320.

[7]Quotations from *Classic American Philosophers*, op. cit., pp. 160, 155, 161, 163n.

[8]Cf. I. M. Bochenski, *Contemporary European Philosophy*, University of California Press, 1961, p. 136 (also for bibliography).

[9]The English translation of his main work, *Being and Time*, was published by Harper, New York, 1962. My references are from the 7th German ed., Tubingen, M. Niemeyer Verlag, 1953, pp. 28ff.

[10]Cf. Bochenski, op. cit., p. 215.

[11]An astonishingly close analogy between the formulation of the four antinomies of the dialectical reason by Kant and the same basic structure of the four groups of "views" (*diṭṭhi*) in the *Brahma-jāla-suttam* (D. 1) has been singled out in my papers, Dependence of punar-bhava on karma in Buddhist philosophy" and "My Approach to Indian Philosopy" in *Indian Philosophical Annuals*, vols. I & II, 1965, 1966, under my lay name Chedomil Velyachich.

[12]Cf. Bochenski, op. cit., p. 183.

[13]Jean Wahl, *A Short History of Existentialism*, N. Y., The Philosophical Library, 1919, p. 2.

[14]N. Berdyaev, *The Beginning and the End*, Harper Torchbooks, 1957, p. 92. See also discussion contained in J. Wahl's book ref. footnote 13, above.

[15]Op. cit., pp. 116f.

[16]K. Jaspers, *Philosophie*, 2nd ed. Berlin, Springer, 1948, pp. 814, 813. *Man in the Modern Age*, is the title of one of Jaspers' books in English translation (London, 1959).

[17]In his history of *The Great Philosophers*, the chapter on Nāgārjuna is not included in the selection quoted above (footnote 6) in English translation.

[18]Cf. Bochenski, op. cit., p. 183.

[19]Cf. *A Kierkegaard Anthology*, edited by R. Bretall, Princeton University Press, 1951, p. 99 (from *Either-Or*) and p. 346 (from *The Sickness Unto Death*).

[20]Cf. Julian Huxley, *Religion Without Revelation*, London, Watts, 1967, an analysis characteristic for the necessary elimination of elements which an up-to-date definition of religion should not any longer postulate as essential.

[21]*Man in the Modern Age*, p. 142ff., and *The Great Philosophers*, p. 221.

[22]Cf. *The Great Philosophers*, p. 200.

[23]J. P. Sartre, *Being and Nothingness*, London, Methuen, 1966, pp. 615, 576, 565, 87, 92.

THE BUDDHA'S MIDDLE WAY AND WESTERN PSYCHOTHERAPY

by

SHANTI TAYAL

The aim of modern psychotherapy is to cure, ameliorate, and bring relief to those who are afflicted with problems of living, to those who are diagnosed as mentally ill. In this respect, it is a moot question to ask: what is psychotherapy, what is mental illness, what are its techniques, what are its goals, how does it heal, or how effective it is? In other words, by raising these questions, we are asking for a status report on the system of Western psychotherapy.

A review of current definitions of psychotherapy brings out the prevalent confusion in the tasks facing psychotherapy. All the definitions seem to agree on one point, that is, that psychotherapy deals with some kind of solutions and resolutions of problems of emotional disturbances and behavior disorders. There is considerable divergence of opinion with regard to techniques and processes, goals and outcomes. According to Whitaker and Malone (1953), psychotherapy is:

> An interpersonal operation in which the total organismic adaptation of one individual is catalyzed by another individual in such a way that the patient's level of adaptive capacity is increased.

Wolberg's definition (1954) is more descriptive:

> Psychotherapy is a form of treatment for problems of an emotional nature in which a trained person deliberately

> establishes a professional relationship with a patient with the object of removing, modifying, or retarding existing symptoms, of mediating disturbed patterns of behavior, and of promoting positive personality growth and development.

Definitions such as these, although comprehensive and scholarly, do not help us to answer the questions raised earlier. They raise more questions than they answer. Wolberg's definition says that the professional person establishes a relationship with the mentally ill, but entirely sidetracks the questions as to what is the treatment, what kind of relationship, and why this relationship removes, modifies, or retards painful symptoms. In 1934, after raising the same questions regarding psychotherapy, Geraldine Coster concluded, "we are amazed to find that no one seems to know just why analysis is curative." And after 35 years—in 1969—psychiatrist Richard Chessick laments the sorry state of psychotherapy in these words:

> However, as clinical experience accumulates and reading knowledge deepens and broadens over the years, the regretful conclusion forces itself upon the thoughtful therapist: there is simply no consensus on certain vital issues.

Further, he says, "Just stumbling along in psychotherapy happens more often than is admitted." The whole field of psychotherapy is riddled with traditionalism, dogma, and technocratic rigidity.

The subject of techniques and methods of psychotherapy is a veritable jungle, where health-giving herbs grow side by side with useless and, at times, poisonous weeds. One is in a quandary when faced with such an impressive array of therapeutic approaches—Freudian, neo-Freudian, Jungian, Adlerian, up to the present sensitivity training, encounter groups, and nude marathons. These systems have developed a language and vocabulary of their own which is characterized by ambiguities, cliches, and obscurantism. Psychotherapists, it seems, talk in tongues, as if to obfuscate rather than to communicate.

Much of what is done in psychotherapy is a sterile activity, which tends to give an aura of scientific respectability to the task at hand. These vexations of the scientific spirit tend to convey an appearance that the goals of modern psychotherapy are clear and definitive. On the contrary, they are segmental, truncated and superficial, and are based upon an almost chaotic conceptualization of the purposes of human life.

Despite the exaggerated claims and apparent popularity of Western psychotherapy, one notices, in the West, a growing dissatisfaction and disenchantment with its predictions and results.

It is no small wonder that so many Westerners are turning to Eastern philosophies, religions and meditative practices. They find something forceful, something compelling, something relevant in the Buddha's message. They see in Buddhism a genuine path of escape from the trials and tribulations of this life. The Buddha saw the cure for human suffering in a unique psychology, in the understanding of the mind, the heart, and the will. He also showed the way leading to this cure. This path, this way, this technique is known as the Middle Way. He showed his way for good of many, happiness of many, out of compassion for the world.

The Buddha, in his very first sermon, described the Middle Way:

> Monks, these two extremes should not be followed by one who has gone forth as a wanderer. What two ? Devotion to the pleasures of sense, a low practice of villagers, a practice unworthy, unprofitable, the way of the world (on the one hand); and (on the other) devotion of self-mortification, which is painful, unworthy, and unprofitable.
>
> By avoiding these two extremes the Tathāgata has gained knowledge of that middle path which giveth vision, which giveth knowledge, which causeth calm, special knowledge, enlightenment, *Nibbāṇa.*

The Middle Way is the most fundamental principle in Buddhism. This is the path which can lead one to the ultimate goal in life—*Nirvāṇa.* The Buddha's diagnostic and therapeutic insights are discernible in the Four Noble Truths:

The Noble Truth of Suffering;
The Noble Truth of the Origin of Suffering;
The Noble Truth of the Cessation of Suffering; and
The Noble Truth of the Path Leading to the Cessation of Suffering.

The Fourth Principle of Buddhism is the means whereby

the First Principle—*Duḥkha-satya*—is recognized and realised, the Second Principle—*Samudaya-satya*—is known and understood, and the Third Principle—*Nirodha-satya*—is actualized and thereby *Nirvāṇa* attained. It is therefore called the Way, or Noble Way: *Magga* or *Ariya-magga* in Pāli texts and *Mārga* or *Ārya-mārga* in Sanskrit works. (Gard, 1961)

The Noble Truth of the Path Leading to the Cessation of Suffering is simply the Noble Eightfold Path. This Eightfold Path, applied to conditions of contemporary life, is a sure prescription for a happy, well-adjusted life. Its precepts form the three foundations of a mentally healthy life, not only for a Buddhist, but for everyone.

1. *ETHICAL CONDUCT.*
    a. Right speech
    b. Right action
    c. Right livelihood
2. *MENTAL DISCIPLINE.*
    a. Right effort
    b. Right mindfulness—Body—Feeling—Mind—Dharma
    c. Right concentration (*dhyāna*)—Passionate desires discarded—Intellectual activity suppressed and tranquillity developed—Joy, a sensation, disappears—All sensations disappear.
3. *WISDOM.*
    a. Right thought
    b. Right understanding.

This path is a way of life to be followed, practised, and developed by each individual. It is a self-discipline and, if I may say so, a self-therapy of body, word and mind. This is the regimen for self-development. This is the prescription for the prevention of the chronic ills of life. You may or may not have belief. Praying may or may not be distasteful to you. No worship is required; there are no ceremonies.

This path is a way of life—a point of view in action. It does not require us to renounce this world. It only demands modifying our approach and acquiring a different attitudinal set towards life and our environment. Thus, through rigorous self-discipline, it is a road to self-realization.

Therapy "is successful only insofar as it diminishes the recipient's doubts as to his physical well-being, alleviates his concern about his interpersonal securities, and fosters comforting theo-philosophic beliefs" (Masserman, 1971).

BIBLIOGRAPHY

Chessick, Richard D. *How Psychotherapy Heals—The Process of Intensive Psychotherapy*. New York, Science House, 1969.

Coster, Geraldine. *Yoga and Western Psychology: A Comparison*. London, Oxford University Press, 1934.

Gard, Richard A. (Ed.) *Buddhism*. New York, George Braziller, 1961.

Masserman, Jules H. "Techniques of Therapy". *Science & Psychoanalysis*, Vol. XVIII. New York, Grune & Stratton, 1971.

Whitaker, C. & Malone T. *The Roots of Psychotherapy*. Philadelphia: Blakiston, 1953.

Wolberg, L. *The Technique of Psychotherapy*. New York, Grune & Stratton, 1954.

BUDDHISM AND NUCLEAR PHYSICS

by

UPASAKA WU SHU
(Loo Yung Tsung)

New theories in physics reveal the following facts:

The simplest part of matter is, at present, supposed to consist of protons and electrons. Around the electrons there are lines of magnetic force. The influence of these lines is theoretically universal. This may be expressed in another way: the constituents of the universe interact on one another and are inseparable. Thus, the concept of the individual existence of any single object is based on illusion. This is the first fact.

In 'reality', things do not exist in a three-dimensional state, as the majority, including some scientists, believe. Rather, things exist in a four-dimensional state where to the side of *space* is introduced *time*, an important element. *Continuum* is a new unit of measurement in *reality*: Even *space* and *time* are interdependent ! This is the second fact.

From these facts one can see straightway that the properties of nature, *reality*, are definitely beyond our imagination.

In spite of these facts scientists and philosophers are still trying unabatedly to solve the problem of *reality* with their same old instrument: the power of imagination and reasoning. It is certain that they will be disappointed. The only success possible for them is the stating of those conceptual properties of *reality* into mathematical expressions.

Let us consider the source of our knowledge. It can be shown that the knowledge obtained through the process of thinking or reasoning is *relative* and *indirect.* One can only think of *space* and *time* being independent and not interdependent. Thus one is unable to get rid of one's unreal three-dimensional universe, that is, one's conflict with the properties of *reality.*

This writer believes that the three-dimensional universe is actually the projection (or projections) of *reality* i.e., the four-dimensional state, viewed by different observers from different angles, and is analogous to a two-dimensional plan or elevation which is a projection of a three-dimensional building.

Scientists and philosophers are only modifying the projections in order to minimise the error and get nearer the profiles of *reality.* They are only designing but not constructing the building. It is obvious that no matter however full of details and however accurate their designs may be, the building cannot become actual without construction.

It is equally obvious that, to a seeker of truth, the theories of scientists and philosophers are only helpful to a certain extent but are not at all vital. What is more important to him than all theories of science and philosophy is to construct the building of *reality,* with material and labour, so that he could live happily in this building and then see every part clearly.

If one should turn one's direction of observation a hundred-and-eighty degrees, that is, look back at the *direct* source of knowledge—consciousness—one would find a lot of data of an invaluable kind concerning *reality.* But the process of introspection is difficult to master. In order to minimise erroneous and false 'intuition', preparatory training, moral and mental, is essential.

Things are cognised in the process of experiencing them. Experience is preserved in the deepest part of our mind. The function of this part of the mind is so fine and subtle that it is scarcely perceptible to ordinary people. Experience undergoes modification, little by little and from moment to moment. The principle of causality rules these modifications.

In all experience with oneself, the ego, as centre, and material and spiritual elements taken wrongly as individual objects, as environment, a three-dimensional universe is suggested. This false concept produces a centripetal tendency drawing one's attention to the self and individuality. It resembles a free moving element, with initial stress, in a structure. Although there is no external stress yet, the element itself is always under strain. The initial stress represents the force of karma. The strain, the illusive life with suffering. Should this centripetal tendency be properly removed, one would readily be in a universe with four dimensions.

This is actually the Buddhist way of interpreting *reality*. It agrees with modern scientific theories and gives light to the truth-seeker to attain *true knowledge*. The Buddha, the Śākyamuni, is the first Saint in this world who was able to gain insight into the TRUTH. He termed the REAL UNIVERSE, NIRVĀṆA, the four-dimensional state of *reality*. NIRVĀṆA, though it has been explained in many ways, is itself beyond the reach of our speculation.

Using the same parable, one finds that the teaching of the Buddha is a workable or practical design of *reality*, drawn on a transitory map. The details of moral and mental training have incomparable value. They are of greater importance than the philosophic side of the teaching.

The Śākyamuni assures us that every living being, and above all the human being, has the chance and a sufficiency of material to obtain *NIRVĀṆA*. The way of attainment is through moral training and psychological reform.

The Principles of the Buddha lead one to the way of right living, the way that is without contradictions of thought, fallacies of reason and suffering of any kind. This very way may be called 'Genuine Living'. By treading that path, one truly lives and denies death.

The foregoing paragraphs may be summarized as follows:

1. Things exist in a state of relation to one another and not independently.
2. Things interact on one another and are changing every instant.
3. 1 and 2 above show that the state of *reality* is four-dimensional and that its properties are beyond our imagination.
4. Scientific and philosophical theories give us only projections of *reality*.
5. The *direct* source of knowledge is experience. Subjective experience with the ego as the centre of observation gives us a false conception of *reality*. The motive force which causes this seemingly irresistible tendency to misunderstand is called karma in Buddhism.
6. The illusive perception of the universe and especially of a

self that is independent, causes suffering to every creature. The variation of suffering is governed by the law of cause and effect, and works naturally, as a matter of course. The belief in a God or any supernatural being who governs this world, all anthropomorphizing, is just phantasmic.

7. The way to get rid of karmic disturbance is the "PATH TO *NIRVĀṆA*" which consists of moral training; observance of precepts etc., and psychological training; concentration, meditation, contemplation etc. as taught in Buddhism.
8. True knowledge, the aim of philosophy, and virtuous conduct, the aim of ethics, are merely two branches of the one tree of *reality*. Or they may be compared to the two wheels of the chariot that takes a man to *NIRVĀṆA*.
9. To the truth-seeker, right knowledge is the microscope, training is the experiment, and the whole universe a perfect laboratory.
10. The teaching of the Buddha furnishes all that a seeker of truth needs to learn and to follow.

ATOM AND ANATTĀ

by

UPASAKA WU SHU
(Loo Yung Tsung)

Everybody should agree in saying that science is the leading factor that creates modern civilization. The recent discovery of the release of nuclear energy brings mankind to a new age—the so-called Atomic Age. But unfortunately, the first sign that served as an announcement of the opening of this new era was the explosion of a new lethal weapon called the atomic bomb.

Men worry because they are living in an Atomic Age where total annihilation of the whole civilized race is actually possible. They generally cannot but think that they are going along the wrong track and feel that it would be better to give up the deadly energy and enjoy a peaceful, though simpler, life, like that of their ancestors. But history does not allow events to go backwards. As Mr. Arthur H. Compton, authoritative American scientist, said in 'One World or None', "No group of men had the power to prevent the coming of the atomic age". So the only right thing for men to do is to be aware of the serious position where mankind now stands and adjust their thinking and their mode of living in such a way that they may make the best possible use of this new force that has been put into their hands. As a matter of fact, there is nothing wrong with the bomb; what's wrong is with man himself. Furthermore, the truth revealed about the inside nature of the atom has undoubtedly invaluable influence not only upon the field of science itself but upon all other branches of knowledge, psychology, philosophy and even theology. It is our aim to introduce the important facts and new conceptions disclosed by the scientists of today and to compare these analogically with the fundamental principles of reality unveiled and preached by Śākyamuni, the Buddha, some two thousand five hundred years ago.

In 1808, John Dalton propounded the atomic theory. He believed that an element actually consisted of separate invisible and indivisible atoms. He thought of atoms as things having the properties of a billiard ball. In the latter part of that century, great scientists like Michael Faraday, James Maxwell and Lord Kelvin began their work in the development of electrical science. The electric nature of an atom was partly disclosed. In 1913, Niels Bohr of Copenhagen propounded a theory according to which an atom consisted of two parts, a small heavy nucleus surrounded by a large empty region, in which electrons move somewhat like planets about the sun. Around the electrons, there are lines of magnetic force; the influence of these lines is theoretically universal. Faraday symbolized an atom as a star-fish with a small body and comparatively long limbs which entangle the things the limbs contact. This might be put thus: the constituents of the material universe interact with one another and are really inseparable. This concept of the atom has important philosophical significance. Things do not exist individually. The existence of a single object is therefore nothing more than a mental illusion. The universe is simply a process, a system of inter-connected activities in which nothing moves independently of the rest and where all is in ceaseless motion. This is exactly the same in principle, though different in words, as the Buddha's preaching of 'Anicca' which means the impermanent or transient nature of things.

Until the release of nuclear energy, men still had a shady belief in the existence of ninety-four elements, whose atoms were visualised to be indestructible. Yet, as early as 1905, scientist Albert Einstein had foreseen the fact that mass and energy were convertible, and he gave the neat equation: $E=mc^2$ where $E=$ energy, $c=$ the velocity of light, $m=$ mass. It is apparent from the equation that a small piece of matter, if converted entirely into energy, would give an enormous amount of energy. And this equation has been verified to be correct in principle by the atomic bombs which exploded over New Mexico, Hiroshima,

Nagasaki, and near the Bikini Atoll in the Pacific. Thus matter or the atom can be described as a highly concentrated form of energy. The reaction which occurs in an exploding atomic bomb can be expressed in the following:

U-235+neutron=I=Y=N neutrons (U=Uranium, I=Iodine, Y=Yttrium, N=a number); thus a uranium atom breaks up and transforms into atoms of iodine and yttrium. Atom, the original meaning of which is "indivisible", had been finally proven to be divisible. But in ordinary chemistry, the conventional theory of the atom still holds good for most practical purposes. Paradoxically it might be put in the following way: An atom is not (really) an atom; it is called an atom for the sake of convenience. One might notice the startling resemblance here of science with Buddhism if one ever had read the Diamond Sutta in which it is said 'When the Tathāgata speaks of universe he does not mean really universe; he calls them universes only nominally'.

Let us now turn to a field to which scientists pay comparatively little attention, that is, to our mental faculties. Though the psychic functions are much more complicated and subtle than the physical phenomena, yet every sentient being has enough instruments, and material of his own if he only cares to observe and to do his experiment on himself. Our mental or psychic faculties can be divided into two fields: those which function within the field of consciousness, and those which function beyond the field of consciousness. Different psychologists give different terms and definitions of the latter; some call it subconsciousness, while others call it unconsciousness. Yet they generally agree to mean that part of our psychic activities is beyond the perception and control of our conscious mind. As to the content of this field of subconsciousness or unconsciousness, psychologists suggested various terms as primitive inherited impulses and desire, original nature, impulse, drive, urge, instinct, etc. As a matter of fact, science in this particular branch is still in its infancy.

It is a strange fact that the field of subconsciousness, which is in a large part obscure to the men of the atomic age, can be found clearly and repeatedly stated in various Buddhist writings In these writings not only is the theory of mind given but also the physical and mental trainings are shown for getting hold of the seemingly uncontrollable impulses and desires, for uprooting them entirely, and for attaining the state called Enlightenment where one experiences things as they really are, and finally proves the principle of Anattā which means that there is nothing called a personal ego. It is not possible to mention here with any detail the Buddhist philosophy and training of mind, but it might be of interest perhaps, if I explain briefly the philosophy of the Dharmalakṣaṇa School (the "Consciousness Only" or "Perception Only" School).

According to the philosophy of this school, the constituents of the universe are divided into eight faculties (or eight consciousnesses). The first five are the five sensual faculties, i.e., the faculty to see, to hear, to smell, to taste, and to feel. The sixth faculty is the most active one. It consists of practically all the mental functions within the field of consciousness. The seventh faculty is the instinctive grasp or attachment of the ego. And the eighth one is the most important of all. It is sometimes termed the Reservoir Faculty, where the tendencies and energies of all our previous actions and experiences are kept. The seventh and eighth faculties function continuously as the centre of the psychic system, no matter whether a man is in the state of awareness, or of sleep, or is even in the state we commonly call death. Even when all the above-mentioned six faculties have ceased to function, the force of the seventh faculty, or attachment of the ego, is tremendous; it is like the nuclear binding energy of an atom. It causes the arising of the superficial layer, in different forms, in the instinctive desire to live, to propagate, to possess, etc. As a matter of fact, the ego-instinct originates and directs almost all the superficial functions, such as volition, emotion, etc., and even affects our system of reasoning. It distorts our conscious mind and hence creates the illusory picture of the individual existence of "I", "Being", "Things", etc., thus overshadowing the real nature of impermanence and egolessness. Since all the faculties of the conscious mind are more or less affected by the blind attachment of the ego, it might be said, figuratively, that the field of subconsciousness is the nucleus in which the ego-attachment is the binding force. The other mental faculties move around it like the electrons revolving around the nucleus of an atom. The arrangement of electrons in the orbits of an atom determines its chemical properties, so do the conscious faculties like volition, emotion, intellect, etc., of a certain individual determine his personality or character.

It is worthwhile to mention especially the intellectual power of a human being. It has the power of reasoning, understanding and generalizing all the events occurring in experience; thus through this faculty men are able to transmit and interchange their ideas and thoughts, just as the electrons in the outermost orbit make possible the flow of electric current. Another important feature of the intellect is that it is the least affected by the influence of the ego-instinct. On the contrary, through reasoning and contemplation it even possesses the power of self-realizing the truth of egolessness. It is actually by means of this delicate faculty that the detachment of the ego, figuratively speaking the breaking of a psychic atom, is possible.

Induced, perhaps, by the newly disclosed scientific ideas and theories, a scientist and philosopher like William James declared that consciousness was only a function, and one like Bertrand Russell said that such a term as 'mental' does not belong to a single entity in its own right (that is, the imaginary ego), but only to a system of entities. The revival of egolessness foreshadows the possible recovery of their faith in reality which is built upon a rational philosophy closely related to modern science.

But to understand the emptiness of the ego is one thing; to practise, to realize and to live an egoless life is quite another. Einstein visualized the probable release of nuclear energy but the actual bomb came into existence some forty years later. There were people like Śākyamuni and his Arhat-followers, though with aim quite different from the scientists, who declared their attainment of the state of full enlightenment and annihilation of the ego, yet compared with billions of sentient beings they are just as rare as the self-radiating elements, uranium, radium, actinium and thorium, on this earth. It is also interesting to notice that in the Buddhist teaching, everywhere, the principle of the so-called 'Middle Path' or 'Middle Way' can be seen. This principle essentially teaches one to refrain from going to extremes in both physical and mental practices. And it is believed that this principle effectively leads one to penetration and enlightenment. In the process of penetrating into the nature of an atom, scientists found that an atom consists of a complex system of negatively charged electrons widely spaced around a positively charged nucleus. Charged particles (such as protons, electrons, or alpha particles) and electromagnetic radiations (such as gamma rays) lose energy and thus slow down in passing through that field. They discovered finally a new particle called neutron, a particle having no electric extremities, able to penetrate through the orbits and go its way unchecked until it makes a 'head on' collision with an atomic nucleus. Though atomic science and Buddhism seem to be entirely different, yet they are really tackling the same problem of energy and release of energy by breaking the highly concentrated form of energy, the so-called atom in one case, and the ego in the other. And their direction is the same, namely, 'Inward'. Therefore we should not be astonished by the close resemblance between the two. The energy released through the breaking of an ego is not so evident as in the atomic bomb, yet the Buddha's highest wisdom and infinite compassion are very much like the light and heat released from the natural source of atomic energy—the sun.

I have briefly mentioned two of the three fundamental principles of Buddhism, namely *Anicca* (impermanence) and *Anattā* (egolessness). The other important principle is called *Dukkha* (suffering) or the consequence of an egoistic life. These three principles are so important that they are actually considered as the testing-stone of Buddhism. Any theory or philosophy which is completely in accordance with these three principles is justified to be called Buddhistic; and anything not in accordance with the three is non-Buddhistic. From this fact the rational character of Buddhism can be easily judged.

BUDDHIST MEDITATION AND BIOSCIENCE

by

U. Aung Thein

It is interesting to note that, as scientific knowledge about man and the universe increases, more and more evidence is brought forth to substantiate the doctrine of the Buddha. Buddhism is the path of emancipation laid down by the Buddha. It is embodied in the Four Truths which also include the eightfold path. Emancipation implies the complete and utter termination from the cycle of birth and death.

Science is the objective investigation into nature's laws in order to establish generalizations and explanations for observed facts. As the French physiologist Loeb has stated: "The ultimate objective of science is to predict".

The way of deliverance taught by the Buddha can be described as an Experimental and Experiential one. Just as in science a researcher goes step by step, so also in Buddhism one proceeds towards the goal by gradual training and gradually gained knowledge. It is not sacrilegious to question; blind faith will lead one nowhere. A sustained application of righteous thought, word and deed will transform one to noble inertness culminating in a complete and utter termination from the cycle of birth and death.

The eightfold path is categorized into Three Major Divisions: The first, a Triplet, namely Right Speech, Right Action and Right Livelihood, is Virtue; the second Triplet, Right Effort, Right Mindfulness and Right Contemplation, is Meditation:

and the third, a Doublet, Right View and Right Aspiration, is Realization or Wisdom.

In Buddhism, it is taken as a Fundamental fact that all sentient beings are an integrated form of the five '*Skandhas*' viz., Mentality, Perception, Sensation, Mental Activities and Consciousness. These five non-permanent and interdependent components have through their action, sustained and perpetuated, a point instant of a process, resulting in the chain of rebirths since beginningless time and shall continue, until a nullifying counter-action brings it to a state of residuelessness or final emancipation.

Let us examine this five-fold process "MAN"; of which the Buddha said: "In this fathom-long body lie all the mysteries and problems of the universe".

In the *Satipaṭṭhāna* and the *Mahāsatipaṭṭhāna suttas* it has been said that his body is a composite of various organs consisting of liquid and solid materials. Again, in the "*Milinda Pañha*', in answer to the King, the great sage compared the body to a conglomeration of parts and expressed the opinion that there was no abiding entity.

From the anatomical and biochemical points of view, this body is nothing but a composition of organic systems in which chemical processes are undergoing constant transformation. It is like a Servomechanism because, when any one of its parts is disturbed, the entire ensemble feels the effect. The ability and tendency of the body to always return to its normal equilibrium or base line is known as Homeostasis.

To keep the body and mind in a harmonious state is, according to the Buddhist teachings, the prerequisite for the maintenance of Physical, Emotional and Mental health required for meditation.

This harmonious balance of body, emotion and mind is brought about by the practice of virtue, the first Triplet of the eightfold Path. Virtue is described in the *Visuddhimagga* as abstention, volition and non-transgression. Impediments to virtue are anger, malice, hypocrisy, agitation, jealousy, craftiness, resentment, pride, arrogance, idleness, lust, indulgence of mouth and palate, vulgarity, non-practice of restraint of the senses. The states that counteract these are the causes of virtue.

Any of these states produce alterations in the biochemical balance of the body. The more unequilibrated one becomes, the more neurotransmitter substances such as Acetylcholine, Serotonin and Epinefrin are released. These trigger production of many different types of effects on such organs of the body as the thyroid, adrenal cortex, digestive tracts and reproductive organs. For example, when rage, anger or agitation is experienced the production of Epinefrin causes the blood pressure to rise, and cardial output and oxygen consumption to increase.

Other common states that we experience are fear and anxiety. During these states, far more than the normal amount of acid required is excreted into the intestinal tracts, whereby the membrane is attacked resulting in ulcers.

Prolonged states of nervous tension are known to impair the autonomic nervous system in such a way that it influences negatively peristalsis which impairs the digestive functions and elimination. This results in constipation and self-poisoning, thus adversely affecting the physical, emotional and mental health of the individual.

It can be seen why the Buddha stressed the practice of virtue as a prerequisite for meditation. The practice of meditation is impossible when the physical body, emotions and mind of the individual are impaired. One who has practised virtue can successfully pursue meditation, discard the hindrances and can contemplate on reality and finally acquire liberation. These three major objectives can be attained within the Four Jhānas.

Just as in science accomplishment of a goal is gradual and methodical, so also the attainment of the Buddhist goal in meditation is gradual and hierarchical and is closely linked with the physical states of the body.

The adoption of a steady posture, the dwelling of the mind steadfastly without distraction and having intense concentration are the prime requirements for meditation. The Buddha praised highly the method of producing serenity through mindfulness of breathing by way of which he himself attained enlightenment.

Modern researchers have found that subjects during meditation decreased their respiration rate, their consumption of oxygen decreased by about 20% and a reduction of CO_2 output was noticed.

Other demonstrated physiological effects are the reduction of the rate of metabolism, the decrease in lactic acid in blood with concomitant rise in pH and a decrease in the Galvanic skin response.

By overcoming the hindrances resulting in a state of physical and mental tranquillity, together with the practice of skilful concentration, the first *Jhāna* is attained. This state of desirelessness relates to the absolute control of the plane of form. This initial transition is said to be one of the most difficult tasks to achieve by a traveller on the path.

After conquering the first *Jhāna*, the *Jhāni* attempts to conquer the mental planes. This second *Jhāna* deals with the power of concentration, the ability to focus the mental forces. This is known as *Ekkāgathā* or One-pointedness of mind.

One can imagine what tremendous effects would sustained and prolonged meditation have on the brain and its biochemical reactions when it is known to science that ordinary short-time training can effect changes in the experimental subjects.

At WCLA Berkley in 1964, laboratory species exposed to an enriched environment of learning, developed heavier and thicker layers of cortex and greater total activity of two brain enzymes were noticed. They also produced larger cell bodies.

It is common knowledge that concentrated thought and tranquillity produce waves. This state of tranquillity can be sustained through bio-feedback devices.

Mental activities are known to influence the production of RNA which is closely connected with protein synthesis. Both RNA and the protein molecules are suggested to be connected with short and long-term memory. The mental states during the meditative practice can therefore be assumed to influence the production of the specific types of RNA and proteins. Dr. Penfield in his research on brain stimulation has shown that recall of past experiences can be triggered off by electrical brain stimulation. In a similar manner, the *Jhāni* with the power of concentration can stimulate electrical activity in any part of the brain and trigger off memory. Since sentient beings have existed from beginningless time, it is not improbable to conclude that the feature of recall of past lives can be achieved by one who succeeds in the second *Jhāna* through this physical mechanism.

The third *Jhāna* is a state in which the *Jhāni* dwells in Equanimity. He watches with great impartiality things as they arise and fade away. He is in the equilibrated state of energy. He neither is over-strenuous nor over-lax, and he exists as a molecule in its ground state of energy. In this state, one's bodily processes demand the least amount of energy and one is satisfying the major chemical function of life which is to minimize entropy. Entropy is the measure of disorder. The *Jhāni* in this state is free from restlessness, anxiety and agitation.

Reaching the fourth *Jhāna*, the *Jhāni* is in a state of purity accompanied by mindfulness and equanimity. With cessation of pain and pleasure, both bodily and mental, he has at last reached the completely detached and liberated state.

I shall conclude with a scientific example related to meditation. It is known that neural transmission is influenced by the presence of calcium ions. Electromagnetic waves of approximately 7 to 13 cycles per second are produced during meditation. If electromagnetic waves of this frequency are impressed upon the brain, there is an efflux of bound calcium from the nerve cell membranes. Recent space experiments of astronauts in a state of prolonged weightlessness in outer space have induced religious or rather spiritual experiences.

Increased freed calcium ions due to decalcification of the bones circulate in the blood stream and may thus reach the brain.

It is not unreasonable to conclude that both the spiritual experiences of the meditator and those of the astronauts in prolonged weightlessness can be traced to the same physiological phenomenon, namely, the alteration of calcium binding in the neurological system.

To summarize, I have tried to show in this article that the time invariant path of the Buddha is a scientific one. The objective of both Buddhism and Science is to discover nature's laws and ultimately, by following precise techniques, to reach the predicted goal.

The Buddha said '*Ehipassako*' ! Come and see. And the message of this article is Meditate, Experiment and Experience.

BUDDHISM AND COSMOLOGY

by

F. MARK DAVIS

If you enjoy pleasant and interesting surprises, I have one for you. Though not surprising to a Buddhist scholar, what I am about to tell you will come as a surprise, if you happen to be one of those Occidentals who believes that only his culture has a monopoly on scientific knowledge. Rather than keeping you in suspense, I shall reveal it to you now, and give more details later. It is this: Early Buddhist scholars, while the West was wallowing in a Dark Age, were recording facts about the cosmos that are in near perfect harmony with what is known today by the most competent Western astronomers and astrophysicists.

Why, you might ask, were early Buddhist scholars interested in such a thing as cosmology and the structure of the physical universe, if Buddhism is a religion the primary interest of which is human suffering and the extinction thereof? After all, descriptions of the physical universe have little to do with the human predicament.

That is a fair question, and I shall attempt to answer it. If priority should be placed on the nature of man and his destiny rather than on the nature and origin of the universe, an understanding of the latter is useful in that it enables one to know the nature of things as they are. But that is not the only reason. Men are born, they suffer and they die in the impermanent world of natural phenomena. Thus, if this saṃsāric world is man's place of brief sojourn, why should he not learn to understand it?

And attempt to understand Saṃsāra is precisely what the old Buddhist scholars did. It should therefore come as no real surprise that descriptions of the natural world appear in the ancient texts.

Although we are going to treat the macrocosm, in passing, I would like to say a word about the microcosm. For after all, the microcosm is included within the macrocosm. So, it will be enough to say that Buddhism, from its historical inception, has always had an atomic theory, though the Buddha Himself did not elaborate it. He did nevertheless point out that the minutest portion of matter is in a state of constant flux, never the same from instant to instant. Later Buddhist scholars conceived and described the atom in a similar manner.

As for the world extending beyond man's immediate environment, there was much speculation among all ancient civilized peoples. The thinkers of Greece and India demonstrated a remarkable capacity for rational thought, though many of their conclusions amounted to fanciful poetry and little else. As startling as it may sound, it remained for Buddhism, for the first time in the history of human thought, to conceive of a universe meaningfully comparable with that of modern science. To convince you of the truth of this last statement, allow me to tell of a cosmic description that appears in the '*Visuddhimagga*'.

In a certain passage, the text describes the universe as existing in three tiers or stages, the smallest being called the Thousandfold Minor World System. This system can be compared with the modern conception of a single galaxy, with its millions of stars and perhaps inhabited planets. Our Milky Way or M31, in the constellation Andromeda, are two examples. The next tier is called a Twice-a-Thousand Middling World System, and corresponds to galactic clusters such as are known to exist in Coma Berenices, to mention one. While the Middling World Systems consist of up to a hundred or even a thousand galaxies, the final tier is the cluster of Middling World Systems which form the Major World System, which Hannes Alfvén calls a Metagalaxy. Perhaps such a metagalaxy is that which exists in the Big Dipper as its bowl is known to frame at least a million galaxies.

Aside from the quasars, those strange galaxies on the outer fringes of the universe, modern astronomy comes to a halt at the third stage, owing to limited observability—even with the most highly developed instruments. This limitation, however, does not necessarily limit the universe, for it could go on indefinitely. Similarly, the early Buddhist texts do not say that the Major World System is all there is. Rather than making dogmatic assertions as to whether the universe is limited or unlimited, they leave the matter open.

Edwin Hubble classified galaxies according to shape. Of the six hundred that he studied, he placed them in four categories, namely, (1) elliptical, (2) spiral, (3) barred spiral, and (4) irregular or peculiar. Curiously, early Buddhist literature uses the Pāli word '*Cakkavāla*' as one of the synonyms for a World System. Yet, one of the meanings of the word is also 'wheel', suggestive of Hubble's spiral. Other shapes, however, are not mentioned. Comparing a spiral galaxy with a wheel is most appropriate as we know today that many of these cosmic entities not only have wheel-like shapes, but also rotate in a wheel-like manner. In the Milky Way, for example, such rotation carries the Sun and its system of planets around the entire galaxy once every 250 million years. The early Pāli literature, however, is not the only source of Buddhist cosmic conceptions and information on wheel-like structures. Thus, we shall turn our attention to a Mahāyāna scripture which, though using poetical symbolism, reveals many realistic descriptions.

Of Sanskrit origin and known as the '*Garland Sūtra*', the scripture comes to us via the Chinese who call it the '*Hwa Yen Sūtra*'. In it the Bodhisattva Samantabhadra addresses an assembly to which, among other things, he says, "Some (worlds) are shaped like flowers".

Unless we stretch our imagination, no known galaxy resembles a flower. Yet, lest we be too hasty in dismissing this as poetic fantasy, the sūtra could be referring to a very real world system—if we interpret rings as being flower-like. For there seems to be evidence of intergalactic clouds of gas, none of which are observable by optical or radio telescopy. Some astronomers believe that such structures, being billowy and cloud-like, could resemble flowers. These come about when a collision between a galaxy and a gas cloud "blows" the interstellar gas out of the galaxy like a smoke ring. Such gas clouds, astronomers say, may contain billions of stars.

"Some are vast as the ocean", proceeds the text, indicating that many galaxies are gigantic, therefore comparable with the sea.

"Spinning like a turning wheel", begins the next sentence, coinciding with earlier comments on the Pāli "*Cakkavāla*".

A later part of the same sentence reads, "Some are slender", a statement that provides a fairly accurate picture of barred spirals. Such galaxies as these are observable in the constellations Cetus, Pegasus and Hercules; and, one in the last named has the appearance of being extremely slender, with its spirals scarcely perceptible.

"Some are small", continues the line. This is certainly true, inasmuch as Seyfert galaxies are small when compared with, say, the Milky Way or M31. Smaller still are the distant quasars. The light emitting region of quasar 3C273, for example, is less than a light year in diameter; and, at least one quasar may have a central chord of less than a light week.

"For they have countless forms", continues the sūtra, suggesting galactic configurations other than those classified by Hubble. On the other hand, the line may be referring to cosmic units other than galaxies, about which more will be said presently.

"And (they) spin in various ways...
Some worlds are like a glowing wheel",

read the ensuing two lines. Further comment would be redundant, so we pass on.

"A volcano", reads the first part of the next line, a statement amenable to two interpretations. First, however, let us consider the volcano.

Some volcanos erupt with violent explosions, most notably those with craters plugged with hardened lava. Such volcanos —Mt. Pelee in the French West Indies and Lassen Peak in California, are examples of the plug type—when they erupt, blow out the side of the mountain rather than through the plugged crater—often with catastrophic results. Ask yourself, then, what cosmic entity might explode like a volcano ?

Galaxies, of course. And, what gargantuan cataclysmic events they must be ! It seems incredible that an entire galaxy can explode. Yet, such is the fact as revealed by radio telescopy. Certain quasars have also been determined to be actively exploding. Quasar 3C273 displays an ejected body of matter some 250,000 light years in extent, a distance more than twice as long as the Milky Way's diameter. Though the cause of the phenomenon is unknown, it could conceivably be the result of an extremely violent explosion. Then, too, M87 in Virgo is an exploding galaxy, as photographs show an incredible amount of matter being ejected from its nucleus.

Below the galactic level, another significant exploding unit is the star, sometimes in distant galaxies and sometimes in the Milky Way. For now and then, without warning, an extremely faint and insignificant star will suddenly intensify its luminosity a million times or more. Such a star has become a 'nova' or a 'supernova', depending on the magnitude of its brilliance. It would not be an overstatement to say that the most significant supernova in history was observed in the summer of 1054 A.D. Extant Chinese records note that the "guest star", as it was called, appearing in Taurus, shone brightly as Venus at night and was visible by daylight for 23 days. Then, after eighty nights short of two years, the supernova faded from view. Today the Crab Nebula, as the supernova's gaseous cloud is called, is the object of intensive astronomical scrutiny.

The reason for this is mainly owing to the fact that the immense cloud of debris, which produces the nebula, envelopes an extremely diminutive, superdense neutron star, also known as a pulsar. The pulsar, like other similar ones, gets its name from the fact that owing to its unbelievable rotational velocity, the Crab's pulsar appears to be spinning at the break-neck rate of 30 times per second. Eons in the future, the pulsar will slow down, collapse completely and become one of the most fascinating and widely discussed objects in modern astronomy. And, that will be our next topic.

"Lion's mouth" follows "volcano". At first, this metaphor seems to be an enigma; but when we consider the habits of cats, the probable meaning emerges. A lion's mouth devours the flesh of other animals. What celestial object, then, like a lion's mouth, "devours" everything within its gravitational influence? The answer, to be sure, is the black hole. If "lion's mouth" is indeed a metaphor signifying a black hole, let us give this interesting phenomenon closer scrutiny.

Under certain conditions a pulsar may be compressed below

its small diameter, until it has been reduced to a mere six kilometers or less. After that, something quite extraordinary happens. First, however, an explanation.

Light, according to the relativity theory, has mass; therefore it is subject to gravity. Thus, light escaping from a star will be somewhat hindered by that body's gravitational field. The gravity of a star of normal dimension—say 1,600,000+ kilometers in diameter—is not great enough to restrain the escape of light. Contrariwise, if the matter of a star becomes compressed into an extremely dense state, the gravitational force becomes incredibly great. This frequently happens to the neutron core of an exploded star. When such a core shrinks to a radius of a few kilometers, its surface gravity becomes billions of times greater than that of a normal star. The tug of that fantastic force then prevents everything—even light as tenuous as it is—from escaping spaceward. From that moment the star disappears from the universe as a black, and therefore, invisible hole. And, like the mouth of a ravenous lion, it "devours" everything within its immediate vicinity.

Are we certain that black holes do indeed exist? No. Since they are invisible, they are only theoretically possible. Yet, X-ray astronomy has given a tentative indication that they are real. For X-ray observations made by satellites and rockets have revealed a powerful X-ray source in Cygnus, the so-called Northern Cross. Called Cygnus X-1, this X-ray source is located near a supergiant star that is the member of a spectroscopic binary, a spectroscopic binary being a pair of stars not separately visible. The companion star, in this case, seems to be the X-ray source. But, what do X-rays have to do with black holes? Clarification is in order.

If normal binaries are sufficiently contiguous, the gravitational force of each star causes an exchange of matter. On the other hand, if one of the stars is a black hole, there will be no exchange but a one-way current streaming toward the black hole. As the gas from the normal star nears the black hole, a vortical effect will be created in which the gas' movement will accelerate to an incredibly high velocity, owing to the black hole's irresistible pull. As they approach the black hole, the rapidly moving gas particles collide with one another, become extremely hot and create energetic currents of X-rays. Though some astronomers remind us that pulsars also emit X-rays, the aforementioned radiation leads other astronomers to believe that a black hole does indeed exist in Cygnus.

About the lion's mouth, the sūtra makes no further mention. So proceeding, we note that, at the end of the same line, some world systems are described as being shaped like sea shells. A vivid description of a spiral galaxy, about which comment would be superfluous. So, we pass on.

A few lines later we read, "Some worlds are round and others square." An enigmatic line, to say the least. Beyond this strange line, however, we read two lines which appear to be a redundancy, since we have already discussed exploding galaxies and stars. They are:

"Some world-systems remain for but one kalpa,
While others, for hundreds, thousands or an infinity of aeons."

Several lines beyond, we read,

"Many worlds are new or are decaying,
While many others soon will cease to be."

Assuming that "worlds" here refer to stars rather than galaxies, we know that old stars exist—particularly in elliptical galaxies. If the majority of stars in such galaxies are old, then the ellipticals themselves must be old. Contrariwise, peculiar galaxies seem especially to contain many bright young stars but few old ones. This seems to indicate that such galaxies are themselves relatively young. But this is not necessarily true. Why? Because in the interstellar space of any galaxy, gas and dust exist at extremely rare densities. By gravitational attraction and chance collision, this rarefied matter accumulates over countless aeons into a huge cloud. As the cloud grows, bodies coalesce into embryonic stars or protostars. In the Milky Way, for example, certain nebulae—the Great Nebula in Orion, to mention one—are cosmic maternity wards for such protostars. If so, how does a protostar become a mature hydrogen furnace?

With the persistent action of gravity, a protostar becomes more dense. Pressure builds up which, in turn, produces heat. By the time—say 10 million or more years—the protostar's temperature rises to many millions of degrees, and hydrogen nuclei begin to collide with energy sufficient to counteract the repellant electrical force that usually separates them. The impact of these collisions causes hydrogen atoms to unite and form helium. By then, what was a gas cloud has become a full-blown luminous star. Now the star has begun "to live its life"; and, perhaps 20 million or more years later, it becomes stable as the outward pressure from the super-intense heat of nuclear fusion balances the inward tug of gravity. Then, for several billions of years thereafter, the star remains in this state of equilibrium.

"Some world-systems remain but for one kalpa", reads the sūtra. As concerns a large star, this is scientifically sound. For the greater a star's mass, the shorter its life. According to the Indian tradition, a kalpa is a period of slightly less than four-and-a-third billion years. Thus, if a massive star remains for but one kalpa, its life span is indeed short as compared with that of a relatively small star. For it has been said that a star ninety percent less massive than the sun can burn for a trillion years. And that is more than sixty percent greater than the supposed age of the universe. So using poetical hyperbole, such worlds remain for "an infinity of aeons".

Helium accumulates at the star's core as a result of the fusion of hydrogen. When helium has accumulated in abundance, the star begins to age; and age is the precursor of death. Yet, a considerable amount of hydrogen is still present in the star's outer layers, which tends to collapse and become hotter so that it can be fused. As the star begins to run short of fuel, contrary to expectation, it brightens. After most of the star's hydrogen converts to helium, the core collapses owing to gravitation. Simultaneously, the temperature rises until the helium itself begins to convert into even heavier elements. Then the star brightens more, while the outer layers expand to such an extent that if the star has planets, many of them are now swallowed up. Now the star has become a red giant, such as Betelgeuse and Antares. Once more the star shrinks for a brief period, after which it bulges again to red giant size. With most of its fuel now depleted, the star's core remains as a white dwarf, with its outer layers dissipating into space. Eventually, with its fuel entirely consumed, the dwarf cools to a cosmic cinder. On the other hand, the largest of the red giants will become exploding novae, pulsars and eventually black holes.

Though the remainder of the sūtra contains little of cosmological interest, an ensuing line states,

"Many world-systems are full of rock-torn earth
Dangerous and destroying".

While this may be true of probable planets in other galaxies and probable planets in the Milky Way, it has been proven to be true in the Solar system. To be convinced, we need to go no further than the Viking photographs of the forbidding landscape of Mars.

Let us now leave the 'Hwa Yen Sūtra' and turn our attention to what earlier Buddhist texts have to say about the cosmos. In them, we are told that the universe undergoes two major periods of change: expansion and contraction. This view sounds much like the modern model of the Oscillating Universe, a theory accepted by some astronomers while rejected by others.

This model calls for the acceptance of the familiar Big Bang theory, which is treated in detail elsewhere. It will be enough to say, however, that the theory, in its original form, with certain theistic overtones, asserts that the Big Bang occurred once, never to be repeated. The oscillating theory, on the other hand,—we shall ignore the Steady State Theory as it has been proven to be untenable—while accepting the Big Bang, suggests that it is repetitive. The debris flying out from the exploding fireball to form the galaxies, says the original Big Bang theory, will fly out forever. To prove it, say the theory's proponents, one need only to realize that the galaxies are moving away from one another. Yes, say the defenders of the oscillating theory, the galaxies are indeed flying away from one another; but this process will not continue indefinitely. For, eventually the force of the explosion will spend itself, gravity will take over and the universe will close in on itself to form another globe of matter. In time, this will explode once more to form another universe. And, so it has always been. It is likely that there have been countless universes in aeons past and there will be other universes in the future, ad infinitum.

As plausible as the theory of the Oscillating Universe may sound, there are two difficulties that prevent its universal acceptance. Only one, however, need be mentioned here to demonstrate why the theory is not unanimously accepted. It is this. The density of matter in the universe is too negligible to halt its outward expansion. The universe will therefore expand forever, say the opponents of the Oscillating Universe.

Despite this seemingly damaging evidence, all astronomers are not in unanimous accord. So, the question still remains open. Which of the two theories will be accepted, the one time Big Bang or the Oscillating Universe ? Until astronomers are able to answer conclusively, questions like the following will continue to be asked: Did the universe have a beginning ? Will it come to an end ?

From the point of view of science and philosophy, these and similar ones may never be answered. But answered they have been—provided the questions have been meaningful—not by conceptual thinking, but by an insight level higher than the ordinary. How else but by this kind of insight can we account for such accurate, though poetical, descriptions of the universe as presented by the early Theravādin texts and the '*Hwa Yen Sūtra*' ?

The writers, echoing the teachings of the Tathāgata and probably recording their own findings, had neither optical nor radio telescopes, no spectroscopes, no refined mathematics, no technological aids of any description.... It would be easy to say that they were good guessers, but that is out of question; for there are too many accurate descriptions to be the result of mere chance conjecture. We can only conclude that the early Buddhist scholars acquired such knowledge as they did by one method, namely, the development of Enlightened Insight. And that gives rise to the next question: How can we develop this Enlightened Insight ?

It can be done, to use the words of R. G. de S. Wettimuny, by "(stilling the) trafficking in concepts". As such it is stilling abstract and discursive thought, or stilling what Alan Watts called one's "incessant internal chatter". This is the goal at which all Buddhist schools aim, Theravādin and Mahāyāna alike. Again, to use Wettimuny's words, "One has to let his mind rest quietly on things with pointed attention until...light breaks through". Enlightened Insight or 'Satori', as the Japanese call it, can also come about by deep concentration, and this amounts to what most of us call meditation. 'Satori' may come about while one is sitting in meditation, or it may not. When meditation is practised consistently, 'satori' is likely to break through when you least expect it. The break-through may occur when you are washing dishes, when you are sawing wood, or as one Soto Zen Roshi has said, it may come while one is sitting on the toilet. But meditation by itself is not enough. Something else must accompany it.

The Tathāgata taught that insight comes about when the mind has been purged of the Five Hindrances. Unless this is done, you may meditate until the universe coalesces and only be frustrated. These Hindrances, taught the Buddha, are Sensual Lust, Resentment, Laziness, Disquiet and Doubt. All insight flashes into the mind only when one suppresses these Hindrances; and, the Supreme Goal of Enlightenment can only be attained when these five are completely obliterated. The Goal, then, is not readily accessible; but, if you expect to attain it, you must make the effort. Only when this is done can you, or anyone—scientist or floor sweeper —say, like Lord Buddha, "Done is what was to be done; laid down the burden; there is nothing more to come herefrom".

REFERENCES

Alfven, Hannes. *Worlds-Antiworlds*, 1966, San Francisco & London, W. H. Freeman & Co. 103p.

Baptist, Egerton C. *The Supreme Science of The Buddha*, 2nd edition, 1959, Colombo, Sri Lanka. 70p.

Bonnor, W. B. *The Mystery of The Expanding Universe*, 1964, New York, The Macmillan Co. 212p.

Canby, Thomas Y. "Skylab, Outpost On The Frontiers of Space," *National Geographic*, Washington, D. C. 146: 4 (October 1974).

Capra, Fritjof. *The Tao of Physics*, 1975, Boulder, Colorado, Shambala Publications, Inc. 330p.

Chang, Garma Chen-Chi. *The Buddhist Teaching of Totality, The Philosophy of Hwa Yen Buddhism*, 1971, University Park, Pennsylvania & London, The Pennsylvania State University Press, 270p.

Friedman, Herbert. *The Amazing Universe*, 1975, Foreword by Philip Morrison, Washington, D. C. Special Publications Division, National Geographic Society. 199p.

Goddard, Dwight. *A Buddhist Bible*. Edited by Dwight Goddard, 1952, New York, E. P. Dutton & Co., Inc. 677p.

Hodge, Paul W.	*Concepts of The Universe*, 1969, New York, McGraw-Hill Inc., 125p.
Hoyle, Fred.	*Frontiers of Astronomy*, 1955, New York, Harper & Brothers. 360p.
Jayatilleke, K. N.	*The Message of The Buddha*, 1974, edited by Ninian Smart, New York, The Free Press, Division of Macmillan Publishing Co. Inc. 262p.
Linssen, Robert.	*Living Zen*, 1954, Translated from the French by Diana Abrahams-Curiel, Preface by Christmas Humphreys and Foreword by Dr. R. Godel, London, George Allen & Unwin, Ltd., 348p.
Menzell, Donald H.	*Astronomy*, 2nd printing, date not given, New York, Random House, Inc. 320p.
Reichenbach, Hans.	*The Rise of Scientific Philosophy*, paper, 13th printing, 1968, Berkeley and Los Angeles, California, University of Calif. Press, 333p.
Riddle, Oscar.	*The Unleasing of Evolutionary Thought*, 1954, New York, Vantage Press, Inc., 414p.
Senzaki, Nyogen & McCandless, Ruth Strout.	*Buddhism and Zen*, paper, 1952, New York, Philosophical Library, 87p.
Weaver, Kenneth F.	"The Incredible Universe", *National Geographic*, Washington, D. C. 145: 5 (May 1974).
Gore, Rick.	"Sifting for Life in the Sands of Mars", *National Geographic*, Washington, D.C. 151:1 (January 1977).

BUDDHISM, BIOLOGY AND EXOBIOLOGY

by

BUDDHADASA P. KIRTHISINGHE

The teachings of the Buddha are popularly known as Buddhism, which is considered to be one of the world religions. The teachings are both a religion and a philosophy and are observed as a way of life.

Biology is the science of physical life on earth, dealing with the morphology, physiology, origin and distribution of animals and plants. Exobiology means literally outside biology. It is the study of life forms outside our earth.

Before the scientific revolution which began in the 17th century, monotheistic and polytheistic religions believed in a special divine creation of the earth, men and all other phenomena of our world. This mystical assumption was shattered by the advancement of modern sciences like astronomy, anthropology, physical chemistry and by Charles Darwin's theory of evolution.

Life on Planets May Appear or Disappear, Depending on the Environment

In the science of biology, life processes are studied mainly by observation, experiment and induction. With the advancement of biological sciences like biochemistry, biophysics, genetics, etc., the earliest concepts of a theological world were further upset and it was more definitely affirmed that the world functions in accordance with the law of cause and effect. This is, indeed, one of the principal tenets of Buddhism.

Especially, the belief that man was specifically created in the image of God, has no significance in Buddhism. The rapid advancement of the sciences has dispelled this assumption and has given credence to the fact that life on earth was evolved through millions and millions of years from a single-celled organism to the more complex higher forms of life. This is an accepted fact of life today. Of course, the highest form of life on earth is man—*Homo sapiens*.

On our earth, there exists only one basic form of life—from the simple virus to the largest whale, the redwood tree or man, and it is based on proteins and nucleic acid. All forms of life make use of vitamins, undergo the same kind of chemical changes and employ the same methods of liberating and utilizing energy. They seem to vary in detail.

It is believed that life on earth began in the sea and was made of precisely the same chemical elements that were, or are, common in the sea. Therefore, there are no mysterious ingredients or magical items concocted by the stroke of good fortune or an act of God.

Dr. Herbert Wendt states: "The ocean is the mother of life. In the sea's primeval mud lived the first animals. 90% of plants live there even today, and in water every form of life known today originated".

With modern discoveries in biochemistry, scientists are amazed at the inevitable, at the way things naturally are. They have found how some natural materials like clay may act as a catalyst to speed the build-up of complex organic molecules from simpler forms. They have seen how these complicated molecules naturally take shapes they need for life processes.

A protein molecule, for example, is a long chain of thousands of sub-units called amino acids. To be biologically active, this chain has to fold up in one particular way and in no other.

Scientists have realized for some time that the primitive earth, rather a common type of new planet, could be rich in simple organic chemicals. These should include amino acids. The miracle of organic life to them lay in the build-up, from these simple chemicals, of large molecules that have to have very specific compositions and shapes to do their job.

Scientists say that, in nature or in the laboratory, a chain of amino acids has a natural tendency to assume just those forms we see in nature. This comes from residual electrical forces which make the chains take particular shapes rather than random forms. It is claimed that for the amino acids some tend more readily than others to form chains. These seem to be the ones most abundant in living systems.

Scientists the world over believe that, given a soup of amino acids like the early oceans, the emergence of life is virtually inevitable. Dr. Barghoon of Harvard University believes that organic life was a going concern very early in earth's history. He has found fossil evidence of bacteria and algae in the oldest rocks yet known—the fig tree rock charts of South Africa which date from 3.1 billion years ago.

Bacteria and algae already represent fairly advanced life forms. They are as far advanced ahead of first living systems as modern plants are advanced beyond these one-celled forms. There must have been a fairly long evolutionary period during which the early bacteria arose. Since the solid earth dates only from 4.5 billion years, this leaves less than a billion years for the rise of its life forms.

Scientists now claim that, given proper temperature, water, carbon and nitrogen in some form, which was the case in primitive earth, life is almost inevitable.

When the right catalysts came together, the rise of life must have happened in one year. There is no justification for the scientists' views that it took 100 million years.

With the evolution of chordates, with a skeleton and efficient nervous system, the chordates progressed from fish, still resident in the sea, to amphibia and reptiles which adapted themselves to existence on land in search of plant life. From reptiles, birds and mammals evolved and mammals gave rise to primates. From the primates rose nature's dominant animal, homo sapiens, agile and largest brained animal—man.

It must be pointed out that this process of spontaneous life appearance is not confined only to our earth, but is virtually inevitable on any favourable planet in the whole universe.

NATURAL SELECTION AND EVOLUTION

by

BUDDHADASA P. KIRTHISINGHE

What is life? This is a difficult question to answer from the scientific point of view. Professor Rhodes describes life as a series of processes which take place within certain complex levels of organization of matter. The Buddhists, nevertheless, (the Buddha did not speak about the first cause of life) stress cause and effect with regard to the life continuum according to the doctrine of Dependent Origination (see below). It clearly shows how a cause becomes an effect and an effect becomes a cause. According to the Ven. Nyanaponike, however, in the case of mental phenomena, the cause never becomes the effect and the effect never becomes the cause; although an effect may become a condition of various types of phenomena, but never a productive cause. Generally in Buddhism, the terms "condition" and "conditionality" are to be preferred. Likewise in science and philosophy, the terms cause and effect are too great a simplification, but they are still in popular use.

This continuous recurring of birth and death called '*saṃsāra*' has been aptly described as a cycle or wheel. It is inconceivable to ascertain the beginning in such a circle of cause and effect; therefore, with regard to the ultimate origin of life, Buddha declares: "Without cognizable end in this recurrent wandering (*saṃsāra*) a first beginning of beings who, obstructed by ignorance and fettered by craving, wander to and fro, is not to be perceived".

One should not worry in vain, seeking for a beginning in a beginningless past. Life is a process of becoming, a force, a flux and as such necessitates a beginningless past, whether one is an ape or a man.

Nevertheless life, we know, is a unity, and for all their diversity, countless millions of living things over thousands of millions of years have shared this common process. In this lies at once both simplicity and the wonder of life.

A recent investigation of the upper one-inch layer of soil near the American capital showed it contained more than 1,000,000 microscopic animals and 2,000,000 microscopic seeds per acre. It had more than 300,000 species of living plants and 1,120,000 species of living animals, and more than three quarters are insects, while vertebrates or higher animals constitute only 5 per cent. About 20 per cent constituted molluses (snails, etc.) and other arthropods (insects, crabs, spiders and centipedes), and protozoa (unicellular organisms). So there is abundance of life and this is a major factor in the evolution of life. As Charles Darwin showed, it leads inevitably to natural selection. In nature, with overproduction of organisms and an inevitable struggle for existence, there is survival of the fittest—this is the general theory of natural selection.

When considering the influence of Darwin on human thought during the last 100 years, it is worthwhile to distinguish sharply between evolution as an historical fact and the operating theory of modification in descent. It was the first of these that caught the popular imagination and staggered the Victorian Age in the West by its implications for religious philosophy, and in all parts of the world dealt a mortal blow to the traditional and superstitious mythologies with which men of all races have surrounded their ideas about human origins, except perhaps the Buddhists.

In the evolutionary process, the theory of natural selection developed by Darwin was very important. He further showed how modification in the course of descent came about. Living things have evolved continuously and successive periods of time have each been characterized by particular types, levels and assemblage of living organisms.

Julian Huxley states: "The natural system is a genealogical arrangement with acquired grades of differences marked by the terms, varieties, species, genus, family and order. And we have to discover the lines of descent by the most permanent characteristic, whatever they may be and of however slight vital importance."

The familiar framework of bones in the hands, the wings of bats, the fins of a porpoise and of the horse's neck with the same number of vertebrae forming the neck of the giraffe and of the elephant, at once explain themselves on the theory of descent with slow successive modifications.

Since 1900 Darwin's theory was restated in genetic terms which made possible great advances in our understanding of the process of heredity.

In 1866 Gregor Mendel published his famous work on breeding, which strengthened and consolidated Darwin's theory. The other factor that helped in the acceptance of the theory of natural selection, which created new species in nature, was mutation. The exact method of the operation of mutational phenomena is not fully understood yet. The best-known examples of such mutations are the so-called spontaneous variations (the single variation of Darwin) by which new and distinct varieties of plants and animals arise. The laws of mutability are quite different from those of individual variations. The latter are due to hereditary factors.

It is claimed that long before Darwin, men began to reject the biblical story of creation. One by one Darwin developed the great ideas we associate with his name—natural selection, sexual selection, the arguments from domestication, studies in population pressure, the study of geographical variations and isolation; the evidence of comparative anatomy and embryology, the modes of hybridization, the advantages of hybrids and last of all, the analysis of mind and morals. None of these in any way contradicts the Buddha Dhamma.

Darwin maintained that man was derived from a single stock of ape-like animals inhabiting the old world. He maintained that this single stock had been diversified into numerous species or races. They were also adapted or acclimatized (by natural selection) to resist the diseases of the countries they lived in.

That evolution did in fact occur is most vividly shown from the study of fossils. The discovery of fossil bones of animals which could be compared with those of still living creatures is called palaeontology.

It was the doctrine of evolution that first gave a reasonable interpretation of the nature of faunal changes of fossils by palaeontologists and geologists. Series of animals showing evolutionary changes are most convincingly found amongst vertebrate animals. The classical example, unknown to Darwin, is the gradual change of the horse during 40 to 50 million years, from a quite small four-toed creature with primitive teeth to a large one-toed animal with grinding molars, which alone represents the horse family today.

We possess extraordinary knowledge about the history of mammals. It can be shown in the process of gradual change which converts a creature about the size, build and having the food habits of a pig into an elephant. This took place over a period of 40,000,000 years. As the horse and giraffe lengthened their necks in search of food, so the elephant lengthened its face and lower jaw for the same purpose. Julian Huxley shares with Darwin the thought that probably all existing life evolved from one original form.

Professor Hannes Alfven of the Royal Institute of Technology maintains: "The simplest and most sympathetic answer is naturally that God or some other 'force' directed the development towards a certain goal in 'the crown of creation', that is ourselves. Viewed from a larger scale, with the amoeba as the starting point, the perspective appears more natural, but as soon as we look closely at details, we see this conception untenable. The main question is: How does this supernatural intervention take place? For, if the natural laws are, without exception, valid, there is no place left for such an intervention.

"We are beginning to see that the awesome wonder of evolution from amoeba to man, or, for it is without doubt an awesome wonder—was not the result of a mighty word from the creator, but a combination of small, apparently insignificant processes. The structural change occurring in a molecule within a chromosome, the result of a struggle over food between two animals, the reproduction and feeding of the young—such are the simple elements that together, in the course of millions of years, created the great wonder. This is nothing separate from ordinary life. The wonder is nothing separate from ordinary life. The wonder is in our everyday world, if only we have the ability to see it."

Sir Garvin states: "Moreover in the evolution and adaptation of plants and animals, if there was design, purpose, or guidance, it has so frequently led to disaster that it is utterly out of place to invoke providence to account for them".

There is no such entity as a soul (*anattā*) in men or animals. According to the Buddha all things, animate or inanimate, are subject to change. Nothing is permanent; all things come into being and pass away; hence, there is no permanent entity in the form of a soul or self existing in man or in anything else.

All life on earth is interdependent and does not function in isolation. Therefore, man and animals are not self-sufficient and all biological phenomena are impermanent and undergo continuous change and are in continuous flux (*anicca*) and each is conditioned by environmental factors. Everywhere we find conflicts, and these conflicts indicate the unsatisfactory nature of life, or, to use a Buddhist technical term, are '*duhkha*' (suffering, pain and anguish).

The absurdity of the claim of theistic religions that man has a soul—which is said to be a spark of God in man, an unchanging entity—is clearly demonstrated when human organs, especially hearts, are transplanted from one man to another. Dr. Christian Barnard, the South African surgeon who performed the first human heart transplant, predicted that animal hearts and other organs will be used extensively as replacements for the same organs in human beings in the near future.

REFERENCES

Alfven, Hannes.	*Atom, Man and the Universe*, Pelican, 1952.
Huxley, Julian.	*Evolution in Action*, Perennial Library, N.Y. 1958.
Huxley, Julian.	*The Struggle for Life, Present Living Thoughts of Charles Darwin*, Pelican, 1950.
Rhodes, F.H.T.	*The Evolution of Life*, Pelican, 1951.
Rook, Arthur, ed.	*The Origin and Growth of Biology*, Pelican, 1950.
Smith, J.M.	*The Theory of Evolution*, A Pyramid Book, 1969.
Wendt, Herbert.	*The Road to Man*, The World of Science, 1961.

KARMA, REBIRTH AND GENETICS

by

Buddhadasa P. Kirthisinghe

Happiness and misery, which are the common lot of all living things, especially that of humanity, are not, from a Buddhist point of view, rewards or punishments assigned by a God to a soul that has done good or evil. Buddhists believe in a natural law, called "cause and effect", common to all worldly phenomena. Buddhists do not believe in an almighty God and consequently such a natural law cannot be suspended by such a God or even an all-compassionate Buddha.

This law is called '*karma*' in Sanskrit or '*kamma*' in Pāli, the language of the Buddha. In the words of the Buddha, our own '*karma*' or good and evil deeds, reward and punish us. What is '*karma*' ? It is a force, by virtue of which reaction follows action; it is energy which makes it that way out of the present existing life, and new life is an inexhaustible stream continuously flowing forth.

Accordingly Venerable Piyadassi Thera says: "So long as there is will, there is deed. So long as there are deeds, so long is '*karma*' a grim reality, and reward and punishment are no empty words. Desire gives rise to deed; deed gives rise to result; result exhibits itself as new corporeality endowed with new desire. This resilient energy is always transmuted into fresh life, and we live eternally through our lust to live. The medium, however, that makes all existence possible is '*karma*'."

As Dr. Paul Bahlke of Germany states in his 'Buddhist Essays', it is the knowledge of the law of cause and effect, action and reaction, that urges a man to refrain from evil and gather good. A believer in cause and effect knows only too well that it is his own actions that make his life miserable or otherwise.

Man today is the result of millions of repetitions of thoughts and acts. He is not ready-made; he becomes and is still becoming. His character is pre-determined by his own choice. The thought, the act, which he chooses by habit, he becomes.

"Karma is absolutely pitiless and impartial in its working. As a smooth-polished mirror gives back in its smallest detail any picture we may bring opposite its surface, so does '*karma*' with equal exactitude, throw back the consequence of deed upon the doer."

As the Buddha says: "Neither in the sky, nor in the depths of the sea, nor even by entering a mountain cave, shalt thou find anywhere on earth, a state where thou mayest escape the fruit of thine actions".

Freedom from '*karma*' cannot be taught, it can only be lived; it cannot be acquired by learning, it can only be acquired by living. Each individual should make the exertion necessary for his deliverance. In our own human hands lies the power to mould our lives. Others may lend us a helping hand indirectly, but deliverance from suffering must be wrought out and fashioned by each one for himself upon the anvil of his own actions.

Buddhist psychology reveals that unlimited possibilities are latent in man, and it must be man's endeavour to develop and unfold these possibilities. Man is a mixture of good and evil actions. He is always changing either for good or for evil. The changing is unavoidable and depends entirely on his own actions and on nothing else. By our actions we make our character, personality, individuality. Through our actions alone we must change for the better, remake ourselves and win liberation from ill.

It is our own thirst for life, lust for life, clinging to life which keeps this endless play of action and reaction in perpetual motion. So long as we fail to see the true nature of cause and effect, the true nature of moral causation, so long as there is craving and ignorance in us, thus long will we be fettered to this "Wheel of Life". When the cause of a thing is destroyed, the effect automatically eases to be. Sorrow will disappear if the varied rootlets of sorrow's cause are eliminated. A man, for instance, who burns to ashes a mango seed puts an end to its germinating power, and that seed will never produce a mango plant. It is the same with all component and conditioned things, animate or inanimate.

As the shadow follows the form, and as smoke comes after fire, so effect follows cause, and suffering and bliss follow the thoughts and deeds of men. There is no effect in the world around us but has its hidden or revealed cause, and that cause is in accordance with absolute justice. Men reap a harvest of suffering because in the near or distant past, or in the present life, they have sown the seeds of evil; they reap a harvest of bliss as a result of their sowing the seeds of good.

"Who toiled a slave may come anew a Prince
For gentle worthiness and merit won;
Who ruled a King may wander earth in rags
For things done and undone."

Let a man meditate upon this, let him strive to understand it, and he will then begin to sow only seeds of good, and will burn up the tares and weeds which he has formerly grown in the garden of his heart.

Rebirth

Rebirth or survival after death is an accepted fact of life in Buddhism. This accumulated energy or force continues to manifest itself on other and various planes of consciousness. According to the law of conservation of energy and indestructibility of matter, it is certain that in the process nothing is lost. The vitality or karmic force that is lost in our body begins a new cycle of embodiment.

This is life flux (*santati*) that continuously seeks to manifest itself from one sphere of existence to another, and the karmic energy is sustained by force of craving. This is an invisible karmic force.

'*Karma*' is a form of energy which we carry from life to life—both '*kuśala*' and '*akuśala karma*', i.e., both good and bad. When we die our karmic material passes off in the form of energy until it reaches a suitable womb where an ovum and a sperm combine to vitalize it. The father and mother merely furnish material for a new living being. The karmic factor or individual force (*viññāṇa* or rebirth consciousness) is that which conditions a new life. This does not deny the science of genetics whereby a child inherits the characteristics of parents and close relations. An offspring is also moulded by his social environment, yet all these are conditioned by his '*karma*'.

In Buddhism, there are five distinctive domains of existence and, therefore, possibly five ways of rebirth. They are the animal kingdom, the realm of spirits or ghosts, hell, human existence, and '*sakkaloka*' or heavens.

The Science of Genetics

Genetics is the study of physiology of reproduction and the art of breeding plants and animals.

All heredity is transmitted from one generation to another through tiny sex cells called sperms (male) and ova (female). These two join together in the womb, to form a fertilized egg, which grows into foetus and eventually a baby is born.

Father and mother are both important in the transmission of heredity. The nuclei of sex cells contain chromosomes and each human sperm contains 24 chromosomes, half the number contained in a normal cell, and this number varies with other animals and plants.

The fertilization consists of fusion of the nucleus of the sperm with that of the ovum. The fertilized egg cell divides into two, four, eight and eventually into billions of adult body cells. Gregor Johann Mendel identified the unit of heredity as genes. They are living units found in the chromosomes and are in tiny molecular sizes. Each visible characteristic in plants and animals has genes and, as said before, they are carried in the chromosomes of the nuclei of all living cells. Mendel discovered the law of inheritance, as a 3 to 1 ratio in both plants and animals. He also discovered dominant and recessive genes. His classical experiment helped to fortify Charles Darwin's own theories of the origin of species, natural selection and the survival of the fittest in the struggle for existence.

It is now known that genes segregate into half their number in sex cells (sperm and ovum), and are called haploids and recombine in the fertilized egg, to make up a full complement of genes as in the parent cells.

Therefore children in any family may look alike. Yet from a moral, intellectual and emotional point of view, they may resemble each other closely or differ widely. This is what is meant by conditioned 'karma'. Intelligent parents may produce foolish children or vice versa, depending on the 'karma' of both parents and children.

There are interesting case studies of twins, twins from two separately fertilized eggs in the womb in contrast to identical twins born by division of one fertilized egg into two. It is natural for twins born of two separately fertilized eggs to be different and show the same hereditary differences as ordinary sisters and brothers. But this should not be true of identical twins born by the division of one fertilized egg into two.

It has been observed by a great team of scientists—Newman, Freeman and Holzinger of the famous Chicago University—that as one-egg twins grow older some differences between them begin to appear. One may gain weight a little faster than the other; one may learn a little more easily; one may develop a short temper or otherwise differ from the other. The answer to this departure from true genetics of identical twins is that they are conditioned by '*karma*'—an unavoidable factor.

REFERENCES

Baptist, Egerton C. *The Supreme Science of the Buddha*, Ceylon, 1954.
Carter, C. O. *Human Heredity*, Pelican, 1969.
Dahlke, Paul. *Buddhist Essays*, Ceylon, 1961.
Dunn & Dolzhansky. *Heredity, Race and Society*, Mentor Book, 1960.

THE UNIVERSE AND COSMOLOGY

by

BUDDHADASA P. KIRTHISINGHE

Dr. K. N. Jayatilleke of the University of Ceylon states: "The early Buddhists' conception of the cosmos is in essence similar to the modern conception of the universe. In the Pāli texts that have come down to us we are literally told that hundreds of thousands of suns, moons, earths and higher worlds constitute the minor world system, that a hundred thousand times this is the middling world system and a hundred thousand times the middling world system is the major world system. In modern terminology it would seem, if a minor world system (*culanika loke dhātu*) is a galaxy of which we observe about a hundred million through our best telescopes, the Buddhist conception of time is equally immense."

Modern astronomy recognizes the giant stellar families in the vast expanses of the universe called galaxies through big and strong telescopes. The Russian astronomer Vorontozoff and the British astronomer Fred Hoyle of Cambridge University hold the view of a steady state of the universe. They explain the steady state by the introduction of a hypothesis of continuous creation of matter in the intergalactic space.

Three British mathematical astronomers, H. Bondi, T. Gold and Fred Hoyle, state: "The universe looks the same however far we go in any direction in space." This principle demands that the universe must look the same no matter how far we go forward or backward in time. They further postulate continuous thinning of matter in the space of the universe, caused by continuous expansion and this is compensated by continuous creation of new matter, taking place uniformly throughout the intergalactic spaces.

This postulation does not contradict the universal law of conservation of matter. This point of view provides for the origin and evolution of the individual galaxies. It considers the universe itself as being eternal though with a constantly changing galactic pattern.

It is claimed by astronomers that existing evidence seems to be strongly in favour of an infinite universe. This view is also held by the Buddhists. Professor Hoyle states: "I find my mind forced to assume that the nature of the universe requires continuous creation—the perpetual bringing into being of a new background material". This view is in accord with Buddha's teaching—"nothing is permanent, all things animate or inanimate, organic or inorganic, come into being and pass away".

The chemical constitution of the universe is surprisingly uniform. It is found that about 55% of cosmic material is hydrogen, 44% helium and the remaining 1% is constituted by heavier elements.

A galaxy is as much a system as a solar system. It has form, motion and definite constitution. It exists alone in space, far isolated from others of its kind. Stars and elements continue to be born within it and all the stars within it have sprung up within it.

Our solar system lies within the Milky Way galaxy, with millions and millions of stars and planetary systems. The nearest galaxy to the Milky Way is the Andromeda Galaxy. The Milky Way is one of a group of about 20 galaxies relatively close together. Our sun dominates our planetary system and is a thousand times heavier than Jupiter. All planets lie exactly in the same plane and spacing of the planets outward from the Sun follows a mathematical law, which is applicable to all universal stars and their planetary systems. The Sun itself rotates, completing a turn in about 26 days. The planets all move about the Sun in an almost perfect cycle. This systems is orderly, harmonious and significant. In the universal galactic system, some of its planets bear life and some intelligent life, like our world in our solar system. They must possess the right temperature and atmosphere for such life to exist.

A chronicle of ancient India tells of a small group of beings who came to earth many thousands of years ago in metal crafts, which went around the earth several times before landing. According to the book these beings lived by themselves and were revered by the people. Even today unidentified flying objects (U.F.O.) are observed in our skies throughout the world. Some believe that some of them carry intelligent beings from other worlds, while others dispute this.

Harvard University's Dr. Harlow Shapley and Dr. Edward Purcell believe that one hundred million planets in our Milky Way alone have intelligent life. Professor Gamow of the University of Colorado is of the same opinion. Professor Hoyle of Cambridge and also Dr. Stephen H. Doyle of Rand Corporation, U.S.A., states in his book, 'Habitable Planets for Man', that in our galaxy alone there are likely to be some 640,000,000 earthlike life-bearing planets and that, besides, there are many billions and billions of other galaxies.

It was Dr. John Taylor, Professor of Mathematics at King's College, London, who maintained that there are very likely "millions of planets in our galaxy of the Milky Way alone which have intelligent life on them, and that a proportion of those beings possessing it will be far more intelligent than we are ourselves". Buddhists would agree to that.

Professor Carl Sagan of Harvard University's Observatory, and Dr. I. S. Shklovskii of the Russian Academy of Science, think that it is a reasonable guess that there may be as many as 1,000,000 planets in our galaxy, which not only bear life but bear intelligent life and advanced civilizations. He even wonders whether, perhaps, intelligent life forms from other worlds have visited the earth in the distant past and cites the ancient Babylonian myth to the effect that civilization was founded by a non-human creature of great learning.

Therefore we have references to the '*Brahma Devas*' from other worlds coming down to earth to be of help to those in need, such as the *Bodhisattvas*. The same '*Devas*' visiting the earth to hear the Buddha Dhamma and paying homage to the Buddha before and after his *parinibbāṇa* are stories accepted as true by the Buddhists. The story of the Buddha's visit to Tuṣita Heaven to preach the Dharma to his mother Mahāmāyā is equally believable and valid for the Buddhists.

REFERENCES

Gamow, George	*The Creation of the Universe*, Bantam Book, N. Y. 1969.
Garland, Kenneth, W.	*The Inhabited Universe*, Premier Book, N. Y. 1956.
Hoyle, Fred	*The Nature of the Universe*, Signet Book, N. Y. & London, 1954.
Jayatilleke, K. N.	*Buddhism and Science*, B. P. S. Ceylon, 1960.
Shklovskii, I. S. & Carl Sagan	*Intelligent Life in the Universe*, Holden Day, U. S. A., 1960.
Taylor, John	"Cosmology", *B.B.C. Listener* of June 15th, 1972, p. 786.

GALAXIES AND ŚŪNYATĀ

by

BUDDHADASA P. KIRTHISINGHE

The Buddha, in the '*Sunna Sutta*', declared the emptiness of all worldly phenomena. When organic and inorganic atoms and molecules are split, they generate energy. It can be shown that this doctrine applies to everything in the mighty universe, with its huge galaxies.

Voidness is not nothing, but rather no-thing; no thing that we know by our limited consciousness. What is realised in a transcendental state can only be described as no-thing or voidness.

The heat from the sun is derived by nuclear fusion of hydrogen nuclei to form helium, which takes place only at temperatures of several million degrees.

By spectrographic means, more than two thirds of the known elements have already been identified in the Sun's outer layers, while meteorites contain the whole range of 90 elements from hydrogen to uranium. Therefore, it is safe to assume that the whole universe is made up of the same elements. Hydrogen dominates the universal scene and helium is a poor second. At temperatures ten to fifty million degrees, hydrogen is transformed into helium. In this process, called hydrogen burning, immense heat is given off. At these temperatures helium is transferred into oxygen, carbon and neon, but, owing to heat, these break up as fast as they are made.

As a star grows, a deeper cover consisting of oxygen is surrounded by a mantle of hydrogen. At the center of the star furnace, at temperatures raised further to about one million degrees, magnesium, silicon, phosphorus, sulphur, chlorine, argon and calcium are created. This will illustrate the point in the gaseous state, which is energy composed of subatomic particles, for instance, neutrons, protons and electrons. They combine to form atoms and atoms in various proportions form the elements.

Our solar system condensed to its present form from cosmic gas about four and a half million years ago. A galaxy rotates about its center four or five times in a billion years, while our world rotates round the sun in an year.

In galactic clouds of cosmic gas evolve stars which have their own planetary systems, some of which may evolve life in billions of years. From the cosmic gas, these suns manufacture a few core elements which are present in the universe. This takes billions of years before a sun and its planetary system can be formed.

Professor Berrill writes: "The events that carry the lighter elements through their successive molecular combinations to staggering complexity, responsiveness and capacities of living cells are truly a new order, compared with the molecular chemistry of a star".

Galaxies are formed when uniformly expanding primordial gas breaks up to form millions of separate galaxies and condensation within each galaxy into billions of stars and their planetary systems.

Both Kant and Laplace assumed that our young sun was surrounded by a thin lens-shaped gaseous envelope which later condensed into individual planets. This is the modern view of the formation of our planetary system in which we live. Therefore, in the universe we could expect any other star to have a good chance to procure for itself a planetary system.

There are exploding stars and dead stars. As new solar systems are born, others disintegrate into a gaseous state and may again, after millions and millions of years, reappear as new solar systems. This may happen to our own solar system. Yes, even the inhumanity in us may be responsible for the destruction of our own planet into a gaseous state by exploding superhydrogen devices.

Buddha said that only by detachment can one hope to gain

understanding and this precisely applies today to our science-laden society.

REFERENCES

Lovell, A. C. B.	*The Individual and the Universe*, Oxford Pocket Book, 1970.
Struve, Otto	*The Universe*, M.I.T. Press, Boston, 1968.
The Universe	(A Scientific American Book) 1957.
Śūnyatā Sutta	(Buddhist Publication Society of Ceylon and Pali Text Society of London.)

BUDDHISM AND SCIENCE

by

GERALD DU PRE

Many Buddhists believe that Buddhism deals in one order of truth, while science deals in another. Some go further and believe that Buddhism and science are in opposition. For their part, many scientists, if they think about Buddhism at all, think it is so much nonsense.

I think both Buddhists and scientists misunderstand each other. I would like, by defining both science and Buddhism, to show that Buddhism *is* a science. I believe that when this is recognised, Buddhism will be able to have the standing and influence in the West which it deserves.

We are all, Buddhists and scientists, East and West, human beings, with the same sense receptors, the same limbs and the same central nervous system, and once we were all young. As children we learned by all possible means. We used our sense receptors to gain information from the world, including our own bodies. We looked and listened, felt, tasted and smelt. We acted within our world, exploring, experimenting and discovering, and observing the results of our actions. Finally, we learned to speak and count. We learned to describe what we perceived in symbols—in worlds, numbers and diagrams—and we applied logic to these symbols and constructed in our heads a symbolic model of the universe, including ourselves.

Science means, literally, knowledge. It is simply the recognition that truth, knowledge or understanding of the universe can only be defined as the fullest and most accurate we can achieve by the concerted use of our sense receptors, our limbs and our brain. It is the recognition that understanding involves the use of all human abilities, their cultivation to the greatest degree of finesse and accuracy, and the consideration of all the evidence they provide.

In practice, this involves a great many people carefully observing, bit by bit, the whole universe, experimenting and observing the results, and describing what is observed and done in carefully chosen and standardised symbols, ordered with strict logic. Scientists are children come of age.

Some people at all periods of history have made an occasional acute observation, an occasional discovery, an occasional brilliant piece of reasoning. Science is the bringing together of all such observations, discoveries, descriptions and analyses, and the continual gathering of more, letting them all interrelate with each other, to create the very best understanding of the universe that human beings can attain.

Therefore, popular prejudice against science is unfounded, since it is, in effect, a prejudice against all human understanding. Science, by definition, does not exclude any evidence or method available to human inquiry. It is not a narrow view of the world, and does not use a narrow method. If we experience joy or a deep sense of peace, then this too is evidence for science to take into account.

Religions generally differ from science in believing that there is such a thing as knowledge beyond the human ability to experience it. Philosophies generally use only some of the evidence—that of the intellect—while ignoring observation and experiment. It is the adherents of such religions and philosophies who have to speak of different sorts and levels of truth, or who seek to deny the truth of science.

We know, as most scientists probably do not, that Buddhism is not a philosophy or a religion. It is not an academic discipline, dealing only in words or other symbols, seeking truth on a piece of paper. And the Buddha is not a deity. His teaching did not come to him from any extrasensory source. Remarkable though he was, he was a man, and learned and achieved all he did by the use of his sense receptors, limbs and brain.

We can fairly say, then, that Buddhism deals in the same knowledge as science—that which is humanly accessible.

Prince Siddhārtha, later to be the Buddha, grew up in the Hindu tradition, which was much concerned with human experience—that is, with the way in which human beings experience everything: sensations, perceptions, memories, emotions and symbols. The Hindus had observed that human experience is normally in a state of disorganization, a ceaseless turmoil of doubts, fears, worries, regrets, terrors and longings, quite beyond control. Although this is common to all human beings, in some degree or another, the Hindus saw it as an illness, and developed techniques of tranquillization, rather as we in the West have recently developed tranquillizing drugs.

Prince Siddhārtha, living in comfort, security and plenty, was all the more aware of this disorganization of experience, which gave rise to needless feelings of discontent and unease. He became determined to find a complete cure for this disruption of experience.

His subject matter, therefore, was experience, and his aim was both to understand it, and to cure it of its common malady, which is termed *dukkha*.

We have a memorable account of his struggle to both understand and change his experience. He ignored no information, but subjected all information to searching logical analysis. He rejected no method, until he had tried it to its limits and found it no good. Always he observed his own experience with detachment and ruthless honesty. Eventually, by trying everything, he found the way which worked, and cured his experience of *dukkha*.

He erected upon all these findings and discoveries a carefully stated and logical theory. He left all of his theory and method to his followers, in plain language, with nothing kept back and hidden.

For two-and-a-half thousand years his work has been tested and enlarged by many brilliant men, and in that time many thousands have succeeded in changing their experience in the way he did.

It is this method, this down-to-earth attitude, this spirit of free inquiry, this combining of logical theory, acute observation and practical application, which has made Buddhism so hard to classify in the past. In the light of the definition above, however, it can be seen that Buddhism shares all these things with science. I see no reason, and I have looked hard for one, why Buddhism should not be termed a science. It is not a religion, or a philosophy, but a science.

Since its raw material for study and therapy is experience, it may be termed the science of experience.

The Ancient Greeks, long after the appearance of Hinduism, began to interest themselves in the psyche, which they saw as the essence, soul or spirit which makes a living thing alive. In the seventeenth century England, the term psyche acquired the additional meaning of mind. Later, in the same century, appeared for the first time, the word psychology, a combination of psycho-and-logy, meaning the study of the human soul or mind.

Psychology remained a mixture of religion and philosophy until the nineteenth century. Then it began to become a science, by leaving behind the soul, and even the mind, and concentrating upon the study of experience. People such as Wundt, and later Freud and his followers, took experience as their subject, and studied it by the method of introspection.

The science of experience, therefore, was set up all over again. It would be interesting to know if this was a fluke of history, or whether eastern influences, which were certainly making an impression upon philosophy at the time, played a part in transforming psychology from the study of the soul to the introspective science of experience.

During this century, psychology has been extended to include also the study of behaviour, so that it is now generally accepted to be the science of experience and behaviour. Psychology is still much bedevilled, however, by the fact that its literal meaning is the study of the soul or spirit.

Psychology does not only *study* experience and behaviour, but, like Buddhism, seeks to *change* experience and behaviour. Psychologists are well aware that their science, more than most, should, like Buddhism, give rise to a new way of life, a new philosophy of life, new values, and a new code of behaviour.

Moreover, psychology, like Buddhism, is in a special position, since it studies experience itself, and so the source of all knowledge and understanding, and so of all religion, philosophy and science.

Buddhism and introspective psychology, therefore, cover exactly the same ground, and have exactly the same actual or potential scope. No one need fear, however, that Buddhism will be subsumed under psychology, or explained away by psychological theories.

Instead the acceptance of Buddhism as the science of experience would necessitate the re-writing and re-thinking of the whole history and alignment of psychology. The very name psychology, already obsolete, would become a presumption.

It would need to be recognised that it was the Hindus, and not the Greeks, who laid the foundations for the study of experience. It would need to be recognised that it is Buddhism, and not psychology, which is the science of experience and that Prince Siddhārtha was the founder and father of this science, not Wundt or Freud. Moreover, Prince Siddhārtha's discovery of a radical cure for mental disorganization is sufficient, even without his other contributions, to make him the greatest figure in science, and the greatest it is ever likely to have. Whether or not Buddhism was historically responsible for the rise of scientific psychology, it does not alter the fact that psychology is only a recent extension of Buddhism.

If this was recognized, Buddhism would attain the stature in the West which it deserves, and Western science would be given the theory and therapy of experience which at the moment it so clearly lacks.

BUDDHISM AND PSYCHOTHERAPY

by

GERALD DU PRE

In a previous article, 'Buddhism and Science', I argued that it was not the Ancient Greeks but the Hindus who laid the foundation of the study of human experience, and that Prince Siddhārtha, the Buddha, raised that study to the level of a science. Experience is all the sensations, perceptions, memories, feelings, emotions, images and symbols which we experience from moment to moment.

I argued that Buddhism is a science because it combines observation, experiment and theory in a spirit of free inquiry. Most of all, however, Buddhism is a therapy. Buddhism first came into being because Prince Siddhārtha discovered a cure for mental disorder and (after some initial hesitation) decided to pass on the therapy to others.

In this article I would like to compare Buddhism and Western definitions of mental disorder and mental health, and compare Buddhist therapy with Western psychotherapy. This is a very broad subject and the article can only be a brief survey.

Mental disorder is a general term for psychogenic mental disturbances, that is, disturbances which cannot be traced to any physical cause such as injury, chemical imbalance or deterioration. Under the heading of mental disorder come the phobias, the neuroses and the psychoses.

Psychiatrists and psychopathologists continue to have great difficulty in making any sound classification of the different types of mental disorder. Similarly, it still proves very difficult to establish a standard of mental health. All such standards which have been proposed are highly theoretical and idealistic, and are often influenced by Western cultural values.

Buddhism has already largely solved these difficulties. It has pointed out that everyone experiences a persistent inner voice which interprets what is perceived, justifies actions and reassures the individual about his notion of himself. In most cases, as in Prince Siddhārtha's own case, this experience gives rise to dissatisfaction, suffering and disability. This is the common mental disorder called *dukkha*, which is a sort of common neurosis. Most Buddhists recognize this neurosis in their experience and hope that Buddhism can relieve them of it.

Buddhism does indeed claim, not only to relieve *dukkha*, but also to cure it entirely. Buddhism claims, moreover, that the cure is both total and irreversible, and that it precludes the development of any phobia, neurosis or psychosis, for life !

When the inner voice is stilled, and *dukkha* cured, the resulting state of experience is termed *nirvāṇa*. *Nirvāṇa* is the state of mental health. It is not a theoretical state, existing only as an ideal or an unrealized possibility. Thousands of people have actually attained *nirvāṇa*. It appears also to be the same wherever it occurs, and not contaminated by any local cultural bias.

The Buddhist claims to cure *dukkha* and the claims made for *nirvāṇa* are truly enormous. However, they can be both investigated and tested. It is possible to subject people who have attained *nirvāṇa* to physiological and psychological tests, repeated at intervals over many years. Detailed accounts of the experience of *nirvāṇa* can be collated.

If such investigations and tests provided firm support for Buddhist claims, the way would be clear for *nirvāṇa* to become a world-wide standard of mental health. If *nirvāṇa* is what the Buddhists claim it is, then it *is* a universal standard of human mental health. It only awaits world-wide recognition.

Scientific investigation of Buddhist claims might also lead to certain conclusions about the nature of mental disorder. It might be, for instance, that all mental disorders are only a more extreme form of *dukkha*, in which case a general treatment of *dukkha* might help prevent the development of neuroses and psychoses.

Dukkha is the disorder, and *nirvāṇa* the state of order or health. Buddhist therapy is concerned with the alleviation and cure of *dukkha*, and the attainment of *nirvāṇa*. What, then, is Buddhist therapy, and how does it compare with Western psychotherapy ?

The whole therapy is summarized in a list of headings called the Eightfold Path. It can be divided on the one hand into preparatory or auxiliary therapy, and, on the other, the therapy proper. The preparatory therapy includes a regime of everyday behaviour and mental discipline and an introduction to Buddhist theory and philosophy. The therapy proper is *dhyāna* or meditation.

In the West, psychotherapy is now usually used as a general term for all therapies which aim to alleviate or cure mental or behavioural disorders. Psychotherapy can be divided into two types. On the one hand are 'experience therapies', such as psychoanalysis and the therapies derived from it, which involve interview and discussion. On the other hand there are the behaviour therapies. Increasingly, however, modern psychotherapy is a combination of the two.

When Buddhist therapy is compared with Western psychotherapy, rather close parallels can be seen. It seems that interview and discussion therapy, such as psychoanalysis, parallels the preparatory discussions which usually occur between the guru and the pupil in Buddhist therapy. Meditation itself seems to parallel very closely the most common technique of behaviour therapy. There are some vital aspects of meditation, however, which remain unique to Buddhism.

In psychoanalysis and in the preliminaries to both meditation and behaviour therapy, the therapist and patient discuss the latter's mental problems. The therapist might use any of a variety of approaches, and the patient might exhibit any of a variety of emotional responses and verbal evasions. In all cases, the therapist will probably interpret the patient's problems in the light of his particular theory of mental disorder and its cure.

The difference between psychoanalysis and Buddhist and behaviour therapies is that the psychoanalyst actually seeks to cure his patient by giving him a psychoanalytical interpretation of his mental disorder, and of the ideal state of health he should aspire to. Recent controlled checks, however, strongly suggest that the psychoanalytical therapies alone are virtually useless. Although some people do improve under psychoanalysis, more people improve when given no treatment at all ![1]

Both Buddhist and behaviour therapists agree that verbal insight alone rarely cures any but the most superficial mental troubles. On the other hand, most Buddhists and behaviour therapists are of the opinion that such verbal insight is a useful *preliminary* to the therapy proper. In behaviour therapy, and possibly in Buddhist therapy too, a higher percentage of cures is obtained when such a preliminary is employed.[2] Both Buddhists and behaviour therapists stress to the patient that verbal insight will not *itself* bring about a cure. The greater part of Buddhist philosophy seems to be a particularly thorough exposition of this one point.

What does bring about a cure is the therapy proper, which in Buddhism is *dhyāna* or meditation. I cannot here give a proper account of meditation, but only pick out what appear to be the vital elements of the therapy.

One may briefly say that in meditation, the meditator cultivates a state of muscular relaxation in combination with mental alertness. At the same time, the meditator trains himself not to react, either emotionally or by any muscular movement to any stimulus whatever, whether a perception, or a memory, or an imagined image, or words, or ideas, or any other object of experience.

The most common behaviour therapy is called systematic desensitization. It is used for patients suffering from an irrational dread or phobia. The patient first of all undergoes muscular relaxation. Then he is presented with the thing he fears, such as a spider. This may be the real thing, or (in imaginal desensitization) the patient may be asked to imagine it. This presentation is graded, so that a mild image is presented first, then a little more frightening one, and so on until the object is seen or imagined in its worst aspect. Meanwhile, the patient remains relaxed, learning not to react with emotion or by running away.

The similarities between desensitization and *dhyāna* are plain to see. In both cases, the patient relaxes his muscles yet remains mentally alert. In both cases, he learns not to react to stimuli with any emotional, mental or behavioural response.

It seems clear that systematic desensitization is a specialized version of the technique used in meditation. It is specialized to deal with particular phobias, and so the stimuli involved are highly specific and selected. This technique has indeed proved very successful in curing most phobias.[3]

In meditation, not a particular but a general cure is the goal, and so the stimuli are whatever happens to flash into experience. In the course of meditation, those images will include the stimuli for phobias, obsessions and all other neurotic responses. This technique, too, has proved successful in eliminating such responses.

In the past, the Buddhists and the psychoanalysts have attempted some kind of dialogue, with only limited success. It is possible that a dialogue between Buddhist and behaviour therapists, particularly those specializing in desensitization, might be much more valuable.

There are other aspects of meditation which appear to be unique to Buddhism. One such is *vipassanā*. It is translated as insight, but it is not insight gained by listening to the therapist's interpretations, and neither is it strictly verbal insight at all. It is insight gained during meditation, when no discursive thought is taking place, and when the meditator is in silence.

Psychotherapy appears to have no parallel for *vipassanā*. It is *vipassanā* which differentiates Buddhist meditation most clearly from Hindu meditation. It seems that it is *vipassanā* which plays a vital role in the process which eventually takes *dhyāna* therapy that final step to *bodhi*, or awakening, the moment of total cure.

In this survey of Buddhism and psychotherapy, I have tried to pack in rather a lot. The main conclusions, however, can be summarized as follows:

Buddhism sees 'normal' mental disorganization as the cause, under certain conditions, of an illness called *dukkha*. It has produced a total and irreversible cure for *dukkha*, the cured state being called *nirvāṇa*. If subjected to scientific testing, *nirvāṇa* could prove itself to be an acceptable worldwide standard of mental health.

The Buddhist therapy is called *dhyāna* or meditation. It is only the preliminaries to meditation which bear any resemblance to psychoanalysis, and in fact they bear a far greater resemblance to the preliminaries to behaviour therapy. Meditation itself has close affinities with behaviour therapy known as systematic desensitization. Some aspects of meditation, such as *vipassanā*, however, are still found only in Buddhist therapy, as is the total cure to which they help give rise.

The Hindus founded behaviour and experience therapy. Prince Siddhārtha perfected it. Psychiatry has only very recently begun to rediscover it for the West.

There is a pressing need for Western psychotherapy to gain an accurate understanding of Buddhist therapy, and for Buddhist therapy to acquire scientific recognition. If it did so, it could rapidly become the major world-wide treatment for common mental disorder.

REFERENCES

1. R. P. Knight : *American Journal of Psychiatry*, 1941. Eysenck, 1952; Powers and Witmer, 1951; Cartwright and Vogel, 1960, etc.
2. H. R. Beech : *Changing Man's Behaviour*, Pelican, 1969.
3. Rachman : *Psychological Bulletin*, 1967.

THE BUDDHIST PHILOSOPHY OF SCIENCE

by

GERALD DU PRE

Psychology is not only a study of a particular area of knowledge, but has something to say about the nature of knowledge itself. Similarly, Mahāyāna philosophy is not only the philosophy of Buddhism in particular, but also a philosophy of knowledge in general.

I would like to deal with the Buddhist philosophy of knowledge here, especially the Mādhyamika or Middle Doctrine, and argue that it is in reality a revolutionary philosophy of science.

It is well known that Buddhism recognizes empirical truth—the *saṃvṛti-satya* or relative truth of the Mādhyamika School. Like scientists, Buddhists respect strict logic and exact definition of terms. In Buddhism, as in science, theory is based upon observation and practice. Buddhists, like scientists, are opposed to dogma, and do not have sacred texts which are revered as ultimate authorities. They believe in free inquiry and tolerance, and continually warn, as Newton did, against metaphysics.

But I can hear objections already, from Buddhists and scientists alike. After all, Mādhyamika philosophy claims that relative truth is founded upon *śūnyatā,* a term which is taken to indicate *paramārtha-satya* or ultimate truth, and is yet said to be beyond definition. Thus it might appear that Buddhism takes the religious view that science deals in knowledge of the material world, but that this world is based upon an immaterial yet more real world of the spirit.

Many Buddhists do indeed say that *śūnyatā* represents a spiritual truth quite different from the material truth of science. To this many scientists would reply that the Mādhyamika philosophers, by claiming the existence of ultimate truth, yet refusing to say what it is, are obscuring the whole notion of knowledge, and that their philosophy is at best worthless and at worst pernicious.

It all sounds to the scientist very like Christianity dressed up in Eastern clothes. In the West, Christian theologians of the Middle Ages believed that the heavenly, spiritual world that couldn't be seen was more real than the world that could be seen. They belittled sense experience, saying that it was a source of illusion and error. Later, metaphysical philosophers held essentially the same view. Western philosophers of science agree that the one great innovation of science was the idea that sense experience—the experience which takes place when our sense organs come in contact with an object—is the basis of knowledge. Speculation or dogma about worlds beyond sense experience is metaphysics, which may or may not be true.

However, Buddhism certainly does not put forward this Christian view of truth. In Prince Siddhārtha's home continent of India, the religious doctrines were what we now call Hinduism. Hinduism had a philosophy of knowledge very similar to that which Christianity was later to formulate. Like Christianity, Hinduism believed that sense experience was illusory, and it believed that the real was the invisible Self which lay behind the world that could be seen.

All Buddhists know how utterly Prince Siddhārtha rejected the Hindu view of knowledge, in the basic Buddhist doctrine of *Anattā*. He rejected a religious or metaphysical world which is supposed to exist beyond sense experience; and this world is said to be more real than sense experience. He set up his doctrine of *Śūnyatā* or Emptiness as a radical answer to the Hindu view, and centuries later the Mādhyamika philosophers defended it as such.[1] Thus Prince Siddhārtha and the later Mādhyamika philosophers repeatedly insist that *śūnyatā* is not a metaphysical other world, that it is not mysterious or obscure, that it is not indeed an abstract notion or concept at all. That is, it is not spiritual in any abstract or metaphysical sense of that word.

'The Victors have declared emptiness as the expeller of all

views: but those who hold emptiness as a view they have pronounced incurable'.[2]

Śūnyatā is said to be neither something nor nothing. It is not eternalism, that is, not an everlasting essence behind all phenomena, and it is not nihilism either. *Śūnyatā*, meaning emptiness, is said to be empty even of emptiness. What can it be?

I believe that the Buddhist, in particular the Mādhyamika, philosophy of knowledge is the philosophy of science, because I believe *śūnyatā* indicates experience—*actual experience itself*.

Being real, yet neither something nor nothing, being obvious and immediate, yet impossible to grasp, being all that is said about it, actual experience is surely the only possible thing that *śūnyatā* can indicate. Only this meaning can make sense of the Mahāyāna philosophy. Prince Siddhārtha himself clearly based his teaching upon experience, and Buddhism as a whole is concerned with experience. The Yogācāra and Vijñānavāda Schools specifically identify *śūnyatā* with experience.

However, *śūnyatā* does not mean the *concept* of 'experience', as the Yogācāra and Vijñānavāda Schools seem to suggest. *Śūnyatā* means voidness or emptiness, indicating that what is meant is void or empty of any concept.

Instead, it indicates actual experience itself—the direct experience of sight, sound, taste, smell, touch and conceptual thought. Thus *śūnyatā* is here and now, the actual experience of the words on this page, the light in the room, the feel of the chair, the sound of birdsong outside. To counteract the negative impression given by the word *śūnyatā*, this actual experience is also indicated by a partner term, *tathatā*, or thusness, or suchness, or thatness. *Tathatā* indicates actual experience by simply saying 'that', as one might indicate a room by a wave of the hand.

If *śūnyatā* does indicate actual experience, then Prince Siddhārtha taught the scientific view that experience—what can actually be seen and heard directly—is the ultimate authority. This would make him the first philosopher of science. When Nāgārjuna says that relative truth is based upon *śūnyatā*, he is saying that scientific theory is based upon direct experience, which is exactly the philosophy of science in a nutshell.

Why, then, did both Prince Siddhārtha and Nāgārjuna refuse to say precisely what they meant by *śūnyatā*? It would not have presented much of a problem if they had meant sense experience only. When Western philosophers of science talk of experience, they mean sense experience. But psychologists use the term in a wider sense. They are aware that emotions are part of experience, that words and numbers and concepts too are part of experience. Prince Siddhārtha, the founder of scientific psychology, understood experience in this broad sense.

He had, indeed, an all-inclusive view of experience—a view not only logical but also one he knew directly because of his enlightenment. While it is not too difficult to understand what is meant by 'actual sense experience', it is much more difficult to understand total experience, and quite easy to mistake it for a philosophical position, like idealism. Prince Siddhārtha knew that his followers would make just this mistake.

> '...so...will the brethren become in the future. Those Suttāntas uttered by the Tathāgata, deep, deep in meaning, not of the world, dealing with the void, to these when uttered, they will not listen. But those Suttāntas which are made by poets,...which are a manifold of words, a manifold of phrases,...to these they will listen'.[3]

Such experience cannot be defined because it is all-inclusive and all concepts and definitions are contained within it. There is nothing with which it can be compared or contrasted. To name such experience would be to make it a metaphysical notion, which would rapidly be corrupted into the idea of an essence or substrate lying behind or beneath actual experience. For this reason Candrakīrti called *vijñāna* (consciousness or experience) the Ātman or Hindu Self in disguise.[4] Also :

> 'If there were something non-empty, there might be something termed empty; there is no non-empty something, and so where might there be an empty something ?'[5]

And so, neither Prince Siddhārtha nor Nāgārjuna said just what *śūnyatā* indicates but instead advocated the Buddhist meditation therapy which enables the meditator to understand total experience directly.

Arguing from the standpoint that the only absolute or ultimate truth is experience itself, Nāgārjuna, systematizing Prince Siddhārtha's teaching, said that all words, all symbols, all concepts can therefore deal only in relative or empirical truth.

Scientists entirely accept this limitation of symbols, and are well aware that the highest truth they aspire to is relative truth. They know that the use of any descriptive word is relative to the experience it describes, and that the meaning of any part of a theory is relative to the meaning of the other parts. Theories are conceptual or symbolic models and are constantly adjusted to take account of new information from observation, and constantly reassessed in the light of other theories. One contrary observation can topple a whole theory and give birth to a new one. Scientists build models of the world. They never use words as absolutes or ultimates at all.

Therefore, Buddhists have no argument with science. Neither Buddhists nor scientists deify concepts. Both see numbers and words and logic as useful tools doing a necessary job, not as ends in themselves. Thus Buddhists accept the validity of science, and if they contest any scientific hypothesis, they do so on empirical grounds.

Western science is not just relative truth; it is the soundest, all-inclusive and most successful system of relative truth mankind has yet developed. It is unified, standardized, accumulative and world-wide. Buddhism is in favour of such a system of relative truth—free inquiry rooted in an accumulated body of empirical theory. It criticizes an undisciplined hopping from fact to fact (*vicikicchā*). Western science could help the Buddhists to unify and systematize their dharma and relate it fruitfully to the body of Western scientific theory.

Western philosophers of science might be prepared to agree that Buddhism has put forward the philosophy of science, as I have argued. But they would probably be very doubtful about bringing in the term Ultimate Truth. In their desire to stress that science deals in relative truth only, they have excluded all absolutes and ultimates from their philosophy. They would probably feel that the Mādhyamika philosophy of science, by stressing total experience rather than just sense experience, and by calling it ultimate truth, far from being revolutionary, is unnecessarily 'mystical' and obscure. But it is precisely because it asserts that total experience is the only ultimate truth that the Buddhist philosophy of science is so revolutionary.

In the first place, by having an ultimate as well as a relative truth, it prevents any split into 'material' science on the one hand

and 'spiritual' religion and metaphysical philosophy on the other. It includes both of these aspects in the one philosophy of science.

Just such a split occurred in the West, and we are suffering from that duality till today. Philosophy of science developed very slowly in the West. Science gradually distinguished itself from the religious or metaphysical view of truth and knowledge, but did not necessarily attack that view. Many scientists have accepted religious truth as well, and some continue to do so even today. The view that has gradually emerged is that science deals in a practical, everyday sort of truth—concerned with the workings of the material world, while religion, metaphysical philosophy, poetry, art and music deal in a higher, unchanging, timeless truth concerned with the world of the spirit.

As a result, science has acquired the reputation of being dull and technical and in some way limited and incomplete. People look elsewhere for what science lacks; they look in the most unlikely places, in astrology and alchemy and black magic, as well as in the arts and the established religions, searching for the transcendent, for something changeless that will give them peace. Yet the search is usually in vain.

The Buddhist philosophy of science brings together 'material' and 'spiritual' truth in one unified philosophy. In doing so, it takes the oppressive solidity out of the material and strips the spiritual of all its metaphysics, bringing it back to the immediate here and now.

In Buddhism, the word spirit, if it is used, means total actual experience. It *never* means an essence, a soul or a realm of ideal and immortal beings. If the word spiritual is ever used in Buddhism, it means experiential. It refers not to any particular experience but to total experience, and to the direct understanding of total experience through enlightenment. This same experience which is the basis of science is, in its entirety, the basis of liberation.

In Mahāyāna Buddhism, matter is experience conceptualized. In order to build a conceptual or symbolic model of experience, to speak of the world or the body or the brain, we find it necessary and convenient to consider experience as matter or stuff. The material world is not really heavy and solid and oppressive. It is simply a conceptual model of experience, which is also existing within experience. Thus the term rūpa is used by the

Theravādins to mean matter, and by the Mahāyāna Buddhists to mean form, or conceptual model.

The Mahāyāna philosophy of science takes a world split into spirit and matter and transforms it into emptiness and form, that is, into total experience and conceptual models. And it transforms the religious view of a material world arising out of and contained within a spiritual world, into the scientific view of conceptual models arising out of and contained within total actual experience.

This is revolutionary enough, but the Mahāyāna philosophy of science goes further still. By saying that the actual total experience is the only ultimate truth, it silences all metaphysics both within *and outside* science. It reinforces the fact that scientific truth is never more than relative truth, which is of great value, but it goes further and says that religious and philosophical and any other kind of verbal or numerical truth can also never claim to be more than relative or empirical truth. It denies the validity of any other absolute or ultimate truth asserted by any non-scientific system of thought, since it is impossible for anything at all to exist above, beyond or outside of total actual experience.

Prince Siddhārtha's rejection of the Hindu Self can and should be extended to the God of any other religion or the Absolute of any metaphysical philosophy. God, heaven and hell, 'I think, therefore I am', are all just concepts, just words, contained within experience. All bodies of thought—religions and philosophies and Buddhism itself—are all conceptual models, and are all open to direct testing against experience with all the rigour of the scientific method. Even if heaven and hell were to be scientifically proved to exist, they would remain a conceptual model, and even if someone saw God, this would remain simply part of total experience, and would not in any way transcend it.

Nāgārjuna went even a step further—in the direction of contesting other absolutes in other systems of thought. He did not argue from his own scientific point of view which could, after all, be called simply one point of view among many. Instead, using the dialectical method, he set out to disprove all available religions and metaphysical philosophies *on their own terms*. This is why Nāgārjuna's writings are filled with so much brilliant but difficult philosophical analysis.

He proved that no religion or philosophy could logically

support its assertion that it embodied absolute truth, and so enabled the philosophy of science to claim that it is the only valid philosophy of knowledge.

All in all, then, the Buddhist philosophy of knowledge is indeed a revolutionary philosophy of science, for the following reasons:

The philosophy of science recognizes that scientific truth is relative or empirical and that it is founded upon actual experience. Buddhism also accepts empirical truth, and founds it upon *śūnyatā*. I believe that *śūnyatā* indicates actual experience, and so Buddhism too says that empirical truth must be founded upon actual experience.

I believe that the Buddhist philosophy of science is revolutionary because it is based not just on sense experience, but on total experience, and because it says that total actual experience is the only ultimate truth. This prevents any split into heavy, prosaic, 'material' science, and transcendent, liberating, 'spiritual' religion, philosophy and art. It includes both the 'material' and the 'spiritual', both technology and liberation, in just one philosophy of science. Moreover, it specifically rejects religious and metaphysical truth, and claims that the philosophy of science is the only one and valid philosophy of knowledge.

While the West excells in the systematization and application of empirical truth, the East has, in Buddhism, a philosophy of science which is both older and more advanced than that in the West. The whole history of science needs to be rewritten. Prince Siddhārtha, the Buddha, was the first philosopher of science, giving the East a scientific tradition as old as that of the West, and his major contribution to world philosophy is the setting out of a universal and revolutionary philosophy of science.

REFERENCES

1. T. R. V. Murti: '*The Central Philosophy of Buddhism*', George Allen and Unwin, London, 1960, to which this article is greatly indebted.
2. Mādhyamika Kārikā, Ch. 13.8. Translated in '*Early Mādhyamika in India and China*', by Richard H. Robinson.
3. Saṃyutta-Nikāya II. Ch. XX.7. Pali Text Society.
4. Madhyamakāvatāra, Ch. VI.
5. M.K. Ch.13.7. See above.

BUDDHISM AND PSYCHOLOGY

by

GERALD DU PRE

Textbooks tell us that scientific psychology was founded by Wilhelm Wundt in the latter half of the nineteenth century in Germany. However, they are wrong ! It was founded two thousand five hundred years earlier, in India, by Prince Siddhārtha, the Buddha.

In this article I would like to compare Buddhism and Western psychology. I would like to show that broadly the same philosophical development which has taken place in Western psychology took place long, long ago in the Buddhist psychology of the Abhidhammas. It would also be shown that both East and West have made a unique contribution to psychology and, indeed, to science as a whole.

First, I would like to briefly examine the philosophical similarities between the development of Western and Abhidhamma psychology. In both cases one can trace how the soul becomes the mind, and the mind becomes experience and matter, and in both cases one can see how the ego or self becomes the subject of much dispute.

In both East and West, the religious soul lay at the centre of pre-scientific psychology; indeed, psychology literally means the study of the soul or spirit. The West saw spirit as a sort of semi-physical matter. Milton had difficulty in describing the angels in 'Paradise Lost' because they were made of this wily stuff which, though it existed, yet apparently had no properties or function. In the seventeenth century the Greek psyche, soul or spirit, acquired the additional meaning of mind, and not surprisingly, the mind retained the semi-physical character of spirit. It was thought of, and popularly still is, as a sort of half-way house between experience and matter, more material than experience, yet not as material as an actual organ of the body.

Similarly, in pre-scientific Hindu psychology the *Brahman* or soul became the *Ātman* or Self, and the *Ātman* was seen as an immaterial essence which underlay experience.

Both Prince Siddhārtha and Wundt discarded the soul and the soul-like mind, and replaced it by experience and matter. Prince Siddhārtha repeatedly asserted that nowhere in the *Skandhas*, his theory of psychology, is there a separate and abiding soul—an attitude enshrined in his fundamental doctrine of *Anattā* or No Soul. Instead, the *Skandhas* are clearly divided into *Rūpa*, which means matter, and *Nāma*, which means experience.

In fact, *nāma* is often translated as mind, and this has led some people to suppose that Buddhism accepts the highly dubious Western notion of a semi-physical mind. They have supposed that doctrines such as Mind-Only refer to a sort of semi-physical super-brain pervading the universe and acting as a medium for telepathy and other extrasensory phenomena.

However, it is always taken for granted in Buddhist writings that mind means experience. Also, in Buddhist psychology, as in the Western, extrasensory perception is only a peripheral subject. Buddhism recognizes that there is experiential evidence for it; at a particular stage of meditation one may develop it if one wishes, but it is not central or essential to Buddhist psychology. Moreover, it is taken to be a function of the same material 'mind-base' which gives rise to all the other aspects of experience.

Having made immediate experience the subject matter of scientific psychology, the next question was how to observe it. Generally speaking, the Buddhist method of observation is meditation, which is superficially, rather similar to Wundt's method of introspection. Wundt's introspection, however, has proved to be unsuitable for specific and controlled observation of experience, and is no longer used.

So far as I know, the Buddhists have always been well aware that meditation is inappropriate as a method for systematically observing and analysing experience. Certainly they have always stressed that meditation, to be a truly direct and immediate observation of experience, must not involve any analysis, verbalization or intellectual discrimination of any kind. Instead, the Buddhist psychological theory seems to be based not on specific and limited observations, but on the many insights and accumulated experience gained through regular meditation over a period of many years.

All Buddhist schools, like all Western schools of psychology, accept that experience depends in the first place upon the contact of material sense objects or stimuli with material sense receptors, and the Pāli Abhidhamma also accepts a material base for experience somewhere inside the body. Also, both Buddhist and Western psychology use an atomic theory of matter. In the last few centuries, the sciences of physics and chemistry have greatly advanced our knowledge of matter, and more recently, neurobiology has been able to definitely locate the internal seat of experience as the cerebral hemispheres of the brain.

From what has been said so far, we can see that both Western psychology and the Buddhist psychology of the Abhidhammas share the same philosophical outlook. They both reject any semi-physical soul, spirit or mind and replace it with experience and matter.

All sciences begin by making exhaustive descriptions of their subject matter; this is true of both Western and Buddhist psychology. Simple observation of experience enables one to set down a sound scientific description of what actually happens in experience. However, this kind of observation does not equip one to explain *how* things happen as they are observed to do and any attempt at such an explanation is bound to be only speculation.

Freud and Adler and many other Western psychologists have indeed gone well beyond description, and have produced a great deal of quite unsupported speculation. One large area of speculation is that concerning the ego or self. There is a great variety of very complicated definitions of these; the ego is usually described as a central organizer or hub of experience, while the self is often said to be the basis of individuality—the sum total of past experience which exists in the unconscious.

Prince Siddhārtha was very alert to the difference between what was based on direct observation and what was purely speculative, and he strongly discouraged the latter. As a result, the Buddhist psychology is remarkably sound and compact, and there is very little of the voluminous and uncontrolled speculation which so congests Western psychology. Only one Buddhist school, the Vātsīputrīya or Sāmmitīya School, put forward the hypothesis of a fundamental ego or self, which it held to be the entity which provides continuity between successive mental states. All the other Buddhist schools without exception attacked this hypothesis vigorously and threw it out of the domain of Buddhist psychology. Both the Buddhist and Western critics of a central and fundamental ego have pointed out that it has many of the characteristics of the old soul.

Buddhism says that to believe that an ego plays an essential and fundamental organizing or unifying role in experience is an error, and if such an ego appears to be universal in human beings, *it is only because the error is universal.* On the other hand, Buddhism does not deny a self or ego altogether; nor does any Western school of psychology do so.

In the Buddhist psychology, as in more recent Western schools, the self or ego is seen as simply the learned notion of oneself as a person (*puggala*). Thus 'I' and 'me' are accepted as convenient and conventional terms used in everyday speech and life. But this 'I' is only one notion among many and does not actually organize experience. The Buddhist view, which is supported by modern brain research, is that each aspect of experience organizes itself and full experience at any given moment is simply the sum total of all these aspects added together. This is why the Buddhist theory of experiential factors is called the '*Skandhas*', or 'Groups', 'Heaps' or 'Aggregates'.

Thus far, I have been tracing parallels between Buddhist and Western psychology. However, there are two aspects of psychology, and indeed science as a whole, which are not yet shared by East and West.

A unique scientific innovation made by the West is the establishment of a method which can resolve speculation, whether about the ego or the self or anything else which is amenable to investigation. This is the experimental method. It enables science to move from bare description to a study of the mechanisms—of *how* things happen as they do. It was first used in physics and chemistry, then biology, and more recently it has been applied to psychology.

Whereas descriptive science is just observation, and speculation or philosophy is just logic, the experimental method is the bringing together of observation and logic. The experimental scientist puts forward as many logical hypotheses as he can about how an observed process could actually work. He then devises situations, that is, experiments, in which he can check each of these logical hypotheses against further observation. In this way, out of all the logically possible hypotheses, he discovers which is the right one. He repeats this procedure with each new logical step and so gradually constructs a sound theory of how the observed process actually works. It is a slow method, but a sure one and so much better than endless speculation !

The experimental method has given the world a sound theory of matter and a sound understanding of the human body, although there is still much to be discovered. It has enabled research on the brain to move from anatomy i.e., the description of its composition, to the sorting out of how it actually works. Experimental psychology, in collaboration with neurobiology, is also making progress and is gradually putting speculation to rest.

I believe that to apply experimental findings to the Buddhist psychology also would have a most beneficial effect. It would resolve many philosophical disputes, as between the Early Buddhist and Mahāyāna Schools. It would restore to Buddhist psychological theory its original unity, showing that apparent differences between schools are nearly always only differences in emphasis. And it would make the Buddhist psychology a living and dynamic science once again, part of the mainstream of scientific thought.

Both Western and Abhidhamma psychology are keen to stress that experience and matter are not opposites—set over against each other—but are closely interlinked in a single process. This interlinked rūpa-nāma process is described in the *Skandhas*. Experimental science is able to explore this process in detail: neuro-biologists are exploring the contact of sense stimuli and receptors and the resulting nerve impulses sent to the brain, while psychologists are studying the experience to which these nerve impulses and the brain give rise. They have discovered closer and closer parallels between experience and chemical and electrical activity in the brain, and between particular aspects of experience and particular parts of the brain.

However, there is one vital area in which this research seems to have failed utterly. Despite all efforts, the actual relationship between experience and the activity of the brain remains a complete mystery. While ever closer parallels are found, there is still not a scrap of evidence that there is any physical cause and effect connection between them. It remains a complete mystery how a pattern of electrical impulses in the cerebral hemispheres gives rise to an actual experience, say of redness or of a red rose.

This is a disaster, both for Western and Abhidhamma psychology. Western researchers already suspect that it is a philosophical disaster rather than a failure of the experimental method. They have tried to discover where the existing experience-matter philosophy fails, but as yet without much success. Some have suggested the mystical solution that the electrical activity *is* the actual experience, but experience itself rebels against such an idea, and it is hard to accept this save by an act of faith. Experience and matter seem to be irrevocably separate after all; psychology is more or less back where it began.

Fortunately, this is a philosophical problem which has already been solved. When the Abhidhamma psychology was reaching the limits of its experience-matter philosophy, a new and vigorous school of Buddhism, called the Mahāyāna, was established. This contained, in its Mādhyamika School, a whole new branch of psychology, which was concerned, not with adding to existing knowledge, but with investigating *the nature of knowledge itself*. This is Buddhism's unique contribution to science—a new branch of psychology dedicated to sorting out a comprehensive philosophy of science. Nāgārjuna, and the other Mādhyamika philosophers, asked what experience and matter actually *were* before seeking to explain the relationship between them and discovered that the experience-matter division had been wrongly stated from the start.

Nāgārjuna made the clear assertion that the proper division was not between experience and matter but between actual experience and its conceptualization.

Actual experience itself is total, so absolute, and Nāgārjuna called it the Absolute Truth. It is actual experience just as it is, and so it is also called *śūnya-tathatā* or empty suchness. Concepts too are part of actual experience when seen just as they are in their empty suchness.

But concepts, as well as being bits of actual experience in their own right, also represent or symbolize other aspects of actual experience. Thus the word '*red*' is a squiggle on the page or a sound in the throat, quite different from the colour red, but it also *represents* the colour red. Nāgārjuna called all concepts Relative Truth, because they have meaning only relative to experience or to each other.

In the light of this distinction between actual experience and its conceptualization, experience and matter are both seen to be concepts. The Buddhist word for experience is *nāma*, which literally means name, and the Mahāyānists stress both these meanings, indicating that experience is only a *name* for actual experience, and no more than that. As for matter, this is the meaning given in the Abhidhammas to the word *rūpa*, but the Mahāyānists use the alternative meaning 'form' or conceptual model. Matter is only what we call experience when we conceive of it as a world composed of things and processes. But such a world is a conceptual representation or model of experience, and so matter is in fact *a conceptual model contained within actual experience.*

The Mahāyāna School, as the study of total actual experience, of actual experience and conceptual models, is able to give psychology and all other sciences a sound philosophical base. It makes clear that any science is the observation, followed by conceptualization, of some aspect of actual experience.

Western and the Abhidhamma psychology are therefore not different from any other science: they study an aspect of actual experience, and by conceptualizing it, make it a 'material' process. They contribute to the building up of a single scientific model of the entire universe. They accept the conceptual model of a world containing individual people with individual experiences derived from the world around them and lodged in their brains.

It is *within this model* that the *concept* of experience, as a process taking place within an individual, proves to be synonymous with the neurobiologist's *concept* of the processes that occur in that person's brain. Experience and the activity of the cerebral hemispheres *are* one and the same thing, *within the model.* But this brain activity is not the same as *actual* experience. A pattern of electrical impulses is not the same as the actual experience of a red rose. To say so is to cut right across the distinction between actual experience and conceptual models. The brain activity isn't actual experience because *brain activity is a concept which exists within actual experience* !

Here, this very brief account of the relationship between the Buddhist and Western psychology must come to an end. I hope I have been able to show how the philosophical development of modern psychology only repeats that which took place more than two thousand years ago in the Buddhist psychology of the Abhidhammas. Only in one respect has Western psychology advanced beyond the Abhidhamma psychology, and that is in its adoption of the experimental method. This method has enabled Western psychology to move from description of the process of experience to an account of how this process, and the brain, actually work; the adoption of the experimental method would enable the Abhidhamma psychology to do the same and so become a dynamic science once again. Buddhism's unique contribution is the Mahāyāna School, a whole new branch of psychology which deals with the philosophy of science. It has solved the philosophical problems which beset the Abhidhamma psychology and which beset Western psychology even today.

SCIENCE AND THE SKANDHAS

by

GERALD DU PRE

The *Skandhas* (Pāli: *Khandhas*) constitute Buddhist theory of psychology. This theory analyses the process of consciousness or experience into its component parts, and lists them under the five headings of *Rūpa*, *Vedanā*, *Saññā* (Sanskrit: *Saṃjñā*), *Saṅkhāra* (Sanskrit: *Saṃskāra*) and *Viññāṇa* (Sanskrit: *Vijñāna*). Over the years, the Buddhist psychologists expanded these five headings into a formidable theory which is set out in detail in the voluminous Abhidhammas of the Pāli Canon and of the Sarvāstivāda School, and also in the writings of the later Yogācāra School.

In this article, I would like to give a brief account of the *Skandhas* in the light of modern scientific knowledge. The *Skandhas* are already scientific because they are a description of experience. However, the Buddhist psychologists knew nothing of the nervous system and did not enjoy the benefit of the microscope and the experimental method, which modern psychologists and neurobiologists do. At first I thought that modern science might render the *Skandhas* entirely obsolete but I was pleased to find that this is not the case at all. Instead, modern science, particularly neurobiology, by clarifying *Skandha* terminology and resolving ancient philosophical disputes, reveals that the *Skandhas* are remarkably close to the very latest scientific understanding of the way the nervous system works !

The first *Skandha* is *Rūpa*, which means matter. The Buddhists inherited an atomic view of matter from the Hindus and constructed their own theory of material atoms or *dhātus*. All Buddhist schools believe that there are four primary atoms, the *mahābhūtas*, which appear similar to the early Western theory of the four fundamental elements of earth, water, fire and air. But in fact the Buddhist theory differs from that of the Ancient Greeks in that the atoms or elements are understood in a dynamic way as forces or qualities. This brings it much closer to the view of modern physics. Modern physics and chemistry have now outdated this particular atomic theory and replaced it with a far sounder theory of fundamental particles, atoms, ions and molecules and the periodic table of around one hundred elements. But the important thing is that the Buddhist psychologists understood that the whole world, including the human body, operated at an atomic level.

As well as four primary atoms, there are also in the *dhātu* theory, a number of secondary atoms. Varying numbers of these secondary atoms are found in Buddhist writings, but all schools have ten of them in common. These are the five stimulating atoms or sense stimuli—*gocara rūpa* (Pāli)—and the five sensitive atoms or sense receptors—*pasāda rūpa* (Pāli). Thus the Buddhist psychologists believed in the material and atomic nature of colour (i.e., light), sound, odour, taste and touch, and in the material nature of the sense receptors. This is in line with the modern scientific view and, indeed, there are many similarities in detail too. For example, the Buddhist psychologists, like their modern counterparts, did not define the sense receptors as the eye, ear, nose, tongue and skin, but as 'sensitive atoms' in the *back* of the eye, *inside* the ear, and so on.

These five sense stimuli and five sense receptors are also found listed in Buddhist writings as the *āyatanas*, together with a sixth 'mental stimulus' and a corresponding sixth 'mental receptor'. The mental stimulus is conceptions or thoughts and is variously called either *mano* (Sanskrit: *manas*) or *dharma*.

About the identity of the 'mental receptor' or 'mind-base', there is much difference of opinion among the Buddhist psychologists, even within the same school. This is quite understandable because until relatively recent times, absolutely nothing was known about it, either in the East or in the West. The Ancient Greeks located the 'mind-base' in the midriff, and this was the accepted opinion in the West until only five hundred years ago. The popular theory in the East was that the base of experience was the physical heart. Prince Siddhārtha always resisted indulging in idle speculation, and so simply called it 'that material thing' (*'yam rūpam'*).[1] As a result, most later Buddhist writers called the mind-base *mano*, not specifying what or where it was. But some Pāli commentators reasserted the popular view and identified it with the physical heart, or *hṛdaya*.

It is only quite recently that science has finally been able to answer this question and prove beyond doubt that the base of experience is the cerebral hemispheres of the brain. This clears up a good deal of argument and uncertainty in the ancient Buddhist texts and enables modern Buddhist writers to replace such terms as 'mind-base' and 'heart' with the term brain All Buddhist psychologists would clearly have believed in the brain as the physical mind-base if only they could have seen it as easily as they could see the eye and ear and nose.

To summarize, *Rūpa* covers those aspects of what we would now call physics, chemistry and biology which have a bearing upon psychology. It deals with the material sense stimuli and sense receptors and the brain. The remaining four *Skandhas* are purely psychological, and are put under the collective heading of *Nāma*—mind or experience. The Buddhist psychologists expanded the four *Nāmaskandhas* to between forty-six and fifty-two mental factors ! However, I shall only be dealing with the much smaller number of universal mental factors, that is, those that are involved in experience all the time.

The link between *rūpa* and *nāma* is provided by the important theory of *phassa* (Sanskrit: *sparśa*). This is best known as one of the *Nidānas*, but it is included in the *Skandhas* as the first of the universal mental factors and put under the *Saṅkhāra* heading. *Phassa* is the very modern and scientific view that experience depends upon the contact of three things: a stimulus, a receptor and consciousness.

Since the Buddhist psychologists believe that the sense stimuli and receptors are atoms, they see the contact between them as atomic. Thus far the theory of *phassa* runs closely parallel to the modern view. Modern science is still in the process of exploring this contact and much is still unknown. It is now thought, for example, that the experience of sight depends upon the contact of photons of light with the retinéne II cis molecules in the back of the eye.[2]

However, there is some confusion in the Buddhist writings about just what is meant by the third factor in *phassa*, that of consciousness. There is also much philosophical wrangling over whether or not the contact of all the three is simultaneous and also over whether, it is the sense receptor or the mind (i.e., the brain) which sees and hears and so on. All this makes the basically simple theory of *phassa* seem difficult and obscure.

Fortunately, these obscurities can now be resolved, thanks to the painstaking researches of generations of neurobiologists. We shall presently see that modern science is increasingly able to explain psychology in terms of the functioning of the brain. It is now known that contact of a sense stimulus with a sense receptor does not give rise to sense experience immediately. Instead, it generates an electrical nerve impulse in the appropriate sensory nerve. This nerve impulse passes along the sensory nerve, up through the thalamus, until it reaches the cortex of the cerebral hemispheres of the brain, arriving at what is known as a primary receptive area.

It is here that the third part of *phassa* takes place, a fraction of a second later than the initial contact of stimulus and receptor. When the nerve impulse makes contact with the primary receptive area, it gives rise to sensation. This sensation is, as it were, the raw material of sense experience. It is the crude awareness of light—flashes and sparks—or the crude awareness of sound—buzzing, whirring and clicking, and so on for the other senses.[3]

So we can now say that *phassa* is the contact of sense stimulus with a sense receptor; this contact generates a nerve impulse and the contact of that impulse with a primary receptive area in the brain gives rise to sensation. It is the brain which sees and hears and so on, and not the eye or ear. This bears out the view of the authors of the *Aṭṭhakathā*, quoted in the Aṭṭhasālinī, who wrote:

> 'By the close contact of the object with the 'door' (i.e., the sense organ) one sees by consciousness' (i.e., sensation) 'which takes the sensitivity of the sense organ as its basis'.[4]

Let us continue, for a moment, to trace the route of our sensory nerve impulse because the next stage of its journey brings us to the *Skandha* heading of *Saññā* (*Saṃjñā*). Each primary receptive area passes on the nerve impulses only to its so-called secondary or parasensory area in the brain. Each secondary area receives not only these sensory nerve impulses but also nerve impulses from many other surrounding areas of the brain, the so-called association areas.

It is in the secondary area that the crude sensation gets transformed into a full perception. Perception is the full i.e., meaningful experience of seeing, hearing, smelling, tasting or feeling things. Thus, for example, the crude visual sensation of flashing lights and a patchwork of colours becomes a street full of people, or this book open on your lap. The secondary areas are able to transform a sensation into a perception because of the nerve impulses they receive from the association areas of the brain. Perception is based not just on sensation and the information coming from the sense receptors, but also on information already stored in the brain.

Modern scientific understanding of perception is able to clarify the meaning of *saññā*. While some writers interpret *saññā* as perception, others interpret it as conception, noting, ideation, judgement and discriminating awareness and all of them find justification for their particular view in the ancient texts. Modern science is able to say that *saññā* does indeed mean perception because perception is now known to *involve* conception, judgement, discrimination and so on, all of which are based in the association areas of the brain. The different interpretations of *saññā* are simply different aspects of the very complex phenomenon of perception and it turns out that Buddhist psychologists understood perception remarkably well.

This brings us to our next *Skandha* heading, for there is one important aspect of perception which both Buddhist and Western psychologists treat as a separate mental factor. This is feeling, which is covered in the *Skandhas* by the term *Vedanā*. (The translation 'sensation' is sometimes found, but should be avoided.) On this subject Prince Siddhārtha says:

> 'There are these three feelings, brethren. What three? Feeling that is pleasant, feeling that is painful, and feeling that is neither pleasant nor painful.'[5]

And this view has been borne out by modern brain research

which has discovered in the brain 'centres' for pain and pleasure.

Later Buddhist psychologists retained this basic classification, but distinguished between 'physical' and 'mental' feelings.[6] 'Physical' pain and pleasure (*dukkha* and *sukha*) is that which is caused by stimulation of the sense receptors in the skin and other body organs. The 'mental' feelings are either disagreeable (*domanassa*) or agreeable (*somanassa*), and are aroused by all sorts of stimuli and perceived objects such as spiders or money or clashing wallpapers, which certainly do not cause actual physical pain or pleasure.

This Buddhist classification of feelings remains as good as anything yet put forward by modern psychologists. As for the relationship between 'physical' and 'mental' feelings, and how 'mental' feelings arise, this is still a complex subject, full of unsolved problems. It may be that 'mental' feelings are sometimes memories of past 'physical' feelings which have become associated with a particular object. Thus, if a child is bitten by a dog, it feels immediate pain and it also remembers the pain and remembers it in association with the dog. By a process of generalization it may come to associate this remembered pain with all dogs, or even with all animals, and so find all dogs or all animals disagreeable. This may be how all sorts of perceived objects, originally quite neutral, come in time to be associated with varying degrees of pain or pleasure. However, there are almost certainly other processes at work too and it might be better if we leave 'mental' feelings an open subject and move on to the next *Skandha.*

This is *Viññāna* (*Vijñāṇa*), which means both experience, and also discrimination, in the sense of cutting up a whole into parts, because it divides up whole experience into six parts. These are visual experience, auditory experience, olfactory, gustatory, 'body' and mental experience. We have already seen how modern brain research bears out this sixfold classification. We have seen how each of the five types of sense perception—visual and auditory and so on—is localized in its particular secondary area in the brain, and how non-sensory experience—memories, concepts, symbolic thought and so on—is based in the association areas.

This leaves us only one more *Skandha* heading to deal with, that of *Saṅkhāra* (*Saṃskāra*). This is rightly dealt with last of all because it has been called[7] a 'dumping ground' for all the other mental factors added to Buddhist psychology over the years! Looking just at the universal mental factors, we find that different schools have different lists. Nevertheless, they have the most important ones in common.

Thus, they all include *phassa*, *Manasikāra* (Sanskrit: *Manaskāra*), and *Cetanā* with which I have already dealt. *Manasikāra* means attention and it seems to be equivalent to the modern use of the word. The part of the brain particularly involved here is the reticular formation. But by far the most important mental factor listed under *saṅkhāra* is *cetanā*, and it is this term which completes the Buddhist theory of psychology.

Cetanā is usually translated as volition and is said to be the accumulation, co-ordination and direction of mental activity, leading to the production of *viññatti* (Pāli) which initiate bodily activity—speech and movement.[8] One of the outstanding achievements of neurobiology has been the discovery that *all* nervous activity takes the form of uniform electrical impulses (areas of depolarization). These differ from one another only in frequency and travel along nerve cells. (The British scientists, in particular Lord Adrian, were to the fore in this work.) These nerve impulses are organized mostly at the synapses, the points where nerve cells make close contact with each other. At the synapse, the electrical nerve impulse has to be converted into a chemical transmitter substance which crosses the gap to the next nerve cell where it is converted back into an electrical impulse again. Synapses introduce many variables into the nervous system. As a result, they are able to co-ordinate and direct nervous activity.[9]

This modern understanding of the nervous system enables us to rescue *cetanā* from its abstract generality and equate it with nerve impulses and synapses. Seen this way, descriptions of *cetanā* in the ancient texts are remarkably similar to the modern accounts of how incoming sensory nerve impulses are progressively sorted out at the synapses and finally converted into outgoing motor nerve impulses. These motor nerve impulses, the Buddhist *viññātti*, activate the muscles and the glands and so are responsible for speech and bodily movement and all other aspects of behaviour.

And so our journey along the pathways of experience comes to an end. We have traced the process of experience from sense stimuli to sense receptors, on to sensation and perception, including feeling, ending up with the five sense experiences and the sixth 'mental' or conceptual experience of memories and thoughts. Neurologically, we have seen how a sense stimulus, by striking the respective sense receptor, gives rise to an electrical nerve impulse; we have followed that impulse up the sensory nerve to the cerebral cortex of the brain. Here, we have seen it go first to the primary receptive area, then on to the secondary area and from there to the association areas where it might start travelling back out of the brain and make contact with the muscles and so give rise to behaviour.

This is the account given by modern science and, amazingly, it is also the account given in the Buddhist psychological theory of the *Skandhas*, albeit in a more general and less coherent form. Modern science does not disprove the *Skandhas*; instead it reveals just how close they are to our modern view of the process of experience and the way the nervous system works. It reveals the full profundity of such terms as *phassa*, *saññā*, *vedanā* and *cetanā*, showing how all schools have contributed to this profundity. It resolves old philosophical disputes and leads the study of the *Skandhas* away from philosophical speculation or stale dogma, towards the exciting frontiers of scientific research into the nature of sense stimuli, the structure of the sense receptors and the operations of the brain.

Prince Siddhārtha, the Buddha, did his utmost to set out a scientific theory of psychology and his early followers developed it as far as they were able to. *No other religion possesses such a superb psychological analysis.* For two thousand years, little more progress was made—either in the East or in the West. But now, at last, the *Skandhas* are being expanded and developed once again, in psychological and neurobiological laboratories throughout the world.

REFERENCES

[1]Patthana. Introduction. 8.
[2]Otto Lowenstein. *The Senses*. Penguin, 1966.
[3]Peter Nathan. *The Nervous System*. Penguin, 1969.
[4]Translated by Herbert V. Guenther in *Philosophy and Psychology in the Abhidharma*. Shambhala. Berkeley. 1974.
[5]Saṃyutta-Nikāya. Ch. XXXVI. 1. 1. Pāli Text Society.
[6]Nārada Mahā Thera *A Manual of Abhidhamma*. Buddhist Publication Society. Ceylon, 1968.
[7]By W. M. McGovern in *A Manual of Buddhist Philosophy*. Kegan Paul, Trench, Trubner. London. 1923.
[8]Dr. W. F. Jayasuriya. *The Psychology and Philosophy of Buddhism*. Buddhist Missionary Society Publication. Malaysia. 1976.
[9]Steven Rose. *The Conscious Brain*. Pelican. 1976.

SCIENCE AND THE WHEEL OF LIFE

by

GERALD DU PRÉ

The central theory of Buddhism is the *Bhavacakra*, the Wheel (*cakra*: Pāli: *cakka*) of Life (*bhava*). Actually, this contains three closely inter-related theories: the three basic unhealthy mental factors, the six worlds, and the twelve *Nidānas*. Added to this, there are two co-existing interpretations of the Wheel of Life, as a theory of reincarnation and as a theory of mental disorder. Clearly this is a very wide field and in the comparison with modern science which follows, I shall concentrate on the *Nidānas*.

We find *the twelve Nidānas* on the outer rim of the Wheel of Life. Unlike the *Skandhas*, these are not just a list, but are connected together into a causal chain. This explains the use of the word *nidāna*, which means a link. The technical term for the *Nidāna* theory is *Paṭiccasamuppāda* (Sanskrit: *Pratityasamutpāda*), which means arising (*uppāda*) because of (*paṭicca*) and is usually translated as Dependent Origination.

Many scholars have wrestled with the *Nidānas* and come to the conclusion that they are a rag-bag of obscure terms bearing little relationship with one another. Yet all the ancient schools *insist* that this doctrine is at the centre of the dharma and of the utmost importance. A comparison of the *Nidānas* with modern science thoroughly bears out this opinion of the ancients and reveals that they really are a Buddhist doctrine of major importance.

First I would like to consider, very briefly, the philosophy of *Pratityasamutpāda*, and then, at greater length, the theory itself.

The *philosophy* of *Paṭiccasamuppāda* is the law of cause and effect, said to govern all activity. This law obviously applies to any theory and is particularly associated with the *Nidānas* in Buddhism. By saying that all things are subject to this law (including the Buddhist 'heavens' and 'hells'), Prince Siddhārtha, the Buddha, seems to be making the bold claim that there is no (metaphysical) realm outside the scope of scientific investigation—everything which can be spoken of at all is accessible to a scientific explanation !

As for the philosophy of cause and effect itself, this has always obsessed the Indian mind. The Hindus held a metaphysical view of the matter, which the early Buddhists countered with the more scientific view that it is causality which co-ordinates discrete material and mental atoms.[1] This is very similar to the position taken by Western science in the nineteenth century.

This view has now been abandoned in science because of the revolution in thought brought about by physics in the early years of this century. It was similarly abandoned in the Northern School of Buddhism nearly two thousand years ago, because of the equally momentous revolution in thought brought about by Nāgārjuna and the Mādhyamika School. Mahāyāna Buddhism and modern science hold the same view viz., that it is impossible, and unnecessary, to describe a causal relationship between one thing and another. Instead, all one can do, and all one needs to do, is to observe that one thing always follows another and put this observation to practical use.

This also seems to have been the opinion originally held by Prince Siddhārtha, for he simply said :

> 'When this is, that is; This arising, that arises; When this is not, that is not; This ceasing, that ceases.'[2]

So it seems that two and a half thousand years ago *Prince Siddhārtha held the same practical view of causality which scientists hold today.*

We now come to the *theory* of the *Nidānas*, where we find that there are two interpretations existing alongside each other. According to the first interpretation, it is a theory of *reincarnation.* This offers few problems, for it is worked out in the Abhidhammas and commentaries in very great detail. *All* schools of Buddhism, Theravāda Sarvāstivāda and Mahāyāna, including the Mâdhyamika School, uphold this interpretation and, with the exception only of the later Yogâcâra School, they are all in agreement with one another, even over details.

Reincarnation is a pre-Buddhist belief which Prince Siddhârtha, growing up as a Hindu, would have learned from his earliest childhood. While he came to reject the Hindu Ātman, he continued to believe in reincarnation, as can be seen from numerous statements. His early followers, as also the vast majority of Buddhists up to the present day, have done the same.[3]

It would be possible, and quite valid, to translate the Buddhist theory of reincarnation into the language of embryology, genetics and molecular biology. The theory is not a metaphysical one, as it became in Hinduism, but is plainly biological, with *viññāṇa* defined as the moment of conception in the womb, *nāma-rūpa* as an embryo at the age of four weeks, and so on. But it would be premature to dress it out in scientific garb until its experiential basis has been properly studied.

This basis is memories of past ages and lives, which many people do have, and which Prince Siddhārtha said he could call up whenever he wished.[4] Unfortunately, a scientific study of these memories is only just beginning, and it is too early yet to come to any definite conclusions. *The whole fascinating subject remains wide open, and we can look forward to some interesting discoveries in the years to come.*

The second interpretation of the *Nidānas* is that they constitute a theory of *mental disorder.* This psychological interpretation is held implicitly by all the schools *alongside* the explicit reincarnation interpretation. The original words of Prince Siddhārtha equally support both points of view.

As a theory of mental disorder, the *Nidānas* are an expansion of the first two of the Four Noble Truths, which are suffering (Pāli: *dukkha*; Sanskrit: *duḥkha*) and the cause of suffering. *Dukkha* is actually a very wide-ranging term which includes all the suffering in the world, both mental and physical, together with those things associated with it, such as birth (*jāti*), old age and death (*jarāmaraṇa*); it is represented in the *Nidānas* by these final two headings. The *Nidānas* as a whole are a theory of mental disorder because they trace all this *dukkha* to a complex of *mental* causes.

The two main roots of mental disorder are shown to be *igno-*

rance and emotion. It is ignorance which creates the Wheel of Life and emotion which drives it round.

Ignorance (Sanskrit: *avidyā*; Pāli: *avijjā*; or *moha*) is one of the three basic unhealthy mental factors and is the first *nidāna*. It means not understanding the disordered way the brain works (Theravādin interpretation), and not understanding the nature of knowledge (Mahāyāna interpretation). Ignorance has to do with the activity of constructing theories, hypotheses, interpretations and explanations. Ignorance makes us prone to construct wrong theories; it also blinds us to the fact that all theories are only theories, not ultimate reality.

All this is set out in the first six *nidānas*. Ignorance conditions our mental activity. Consequently, the second *nidāna* of *saṅkhāra* (Sanskrit: *saṃskāra*), operates in a disordered way unchecked by any insight into its own workings. This mental activity, now known to be an electrical activity in the brain, gives rise to the third *nidāna* of experience (*viññāṇa*; Sanskrit: *Vijñāna*), which is sub-divided into the five sense experiences of sight, sound, etc., and the 'mental' experience of concepts. It is because of experience in general, and the ability of the sixth experience to name and analyse the other five, in particular, that a theory of psychology viz., the fourth *nidāna* of *nāma-rūpa*, is able to arise.

Ignorance blinds us to the fact that theories are merely conceptual models based on sense experience. The disordered mental activity which arises from ignorance gives rise instead to a muddling of the roles of sense experience and concepts, which in turn leads to all sorts of wrong and fantastical theories (micchā diṭṭhi). These make our mental suffering even worse. For example, it is the wrong theory of a personal god which causes us, when a loved one dies, to torture ourselves with the question : 'Why did she have to die ?'.

Right theories, like the *Skandhas*, are those which are scientific, that is, which are based upon sense experience. Yet ignorance makes us misunderstand scientific theories too, treating them as an ultimate authority and so regarding matter as an ultimate reality. This is an oppressive view which causes mental suffering all over again.

Nāma-rūpa is another name for the *Skandhas*—the scientific theory of an organism living in an external world of sense stimuli.

This organism, says the theory, has five sense receptors and a brain. These are the fifth *nidāna* of *saḷāyatana* (Sanskrit: *ṣaḍāyatana*) and it is the contact of sense stimuli with these which gives rise to experience. This is the doctrine of *phassa* (Sanskrit: *sparśa*) which is *nidāna* number six. This scientific theory is sound but if it is viewed as something self-contained and ultimate, it becomes nonsense. Contact of sense stimuli with sense receptors and the brain gives rise to experience and experience gives rise to scientific theory. *However, the 'stimuli' and 'receptors' and 'experience' are only formulated within the theory* and so cannot give rise to it at all!

In fact, this scientific theory is not self-contained and is not based on 'experience' in the theory. Instead, the scientific theory is based on, and part of, *actual* experience. It is *actual experience itself* which is absolutely real and is the final authority; it can *never* become part of any theory. The scientific theory is the best theory, but it is still only a conceptual model, built by men and women for their practical use.

What Prince Siddhārtha is saying in the first six *nidānas*, therefore, is that *ignorance ensnares us in all sorts of wrong views which cause suffering, and even when we do construct a sound scientific theory, based on sense experience, ignorance blinds us to the fact that it is still just a theory, for our practical use, and not an absolute truth.*

To speak of 'scientific theories' sounds grand and detached from the point of view of everyday life. But Buddhism says that building scientific theories is simply the only way to acquire accurate knowledge. If we hear a sound in the night, we can respond in an unscientific way by instantly jumping to the conclusion that it is a monster and hide under the bedclothes in terror. Or, we can respond in a scientific way: by listening to the sound carefully, thinking out the most likely explanation, which may be that it is the cat roaming about downstairs, and then (if we are brave!), going downstairs to check if this explanation is right.

Even the grandest scientific theories are the result of following this procedure. They begin with carefully observed sense experience, on which the most likely explanation is based. This explanation is then checked against sense experience again and again till all probable doubts have been removed.

It can be seen that this procedure is a *circular* one, moving from sense experience to concepts and then referring back to sense experience once again. This is the procedure which *must* be followed by anyone making a model or representation. An artist, for example, looks at his subject, draws a few lines on the paper, then refers back to his subject, then draws a few more lines, then refers back again, and so on continually. This simple fact may explain how ignorance creates the Wheel of Life. *The Wheel of Life may be none other than this circular process by which theories are constructed.*

Neurologically, this involves the passage of electrical impulses from the sensory part of the brain across to the concept-forming part of the brain, then back again to the sensory area, making a neural loop. So it may be possible to trace the Wheel of Life to this neural circuit in the brain!

We can see that such a 'wheel' is part of the normal functioning of the brain and we cannot do without it. The circuit itself is harmless but necessary—the problem is how to control the electrical impulses which race around it. Mental suffering is caused when the circuit is activated even when we don't want it to be : when we have a ceaseless and unnecessary mental chatter which we are unable to silence. What causes this ?

The culprit is emotion, the second main root of mental disorder. It is emotion which activates the circuit.

The central position of emotion in the Buddhist theory of mental disorder is sometimes overlooked. Some people think that Buddhism holds the ego to be the root of mental suffering. In fact it is Freud and his followers who have elaborated complicated ego theories and not Prince Siddhārtha. *He* mentions the ego only to deny it, and replaces it with the biological view of a 'sentient being' or organism, who can be fully explained without recourse to an organizing ego. Not only this, Prince Siddhārtha clearly states, in the Noble Truths and in the *Nidānas*, that the root of mental disorder is emotion, whether desire, anger or fear.

In the second Noble Truth he says that the origin of suffering is *taṃhā*. Taṇhā (Sanskrit: *tṛṣṇā*), or lobha or rāga, is one of the three basic unhealthy mental factors and means the emotion of desire. But *taṇhā* can be used in the general sense of 'emotional response', in which case it also covers the final basic unhealthy mental factor of *dosa* (Sanskrit : *dveṣa*) which means the emotion of agression and which is closely linked with fear (*bhaya*).

The role of emotion in mental disorder is elaborated in the *Nidānas*, where it is said that contact (*phassa*) of the appropriate sense stimuli with the receptors in the skin and other body organs gives rise to the seventh *nidāna* of *vedanā*—the feelings of pain or pleasure. The other receptors of sight, hearing, smell, taste and conceptual thought give rise to only neutral *vedanā*, but their perceptions can become *associated* with feelings of pain or pleasure. Because of these feelings, whether directly or by association, we react emotionally to sense stimuli and concepts, which is *taṇhā* or *kāmarāga*, *nidāna* number eight.

Because of *taṇhā* arises the ninth *nidāna* of *upādāna*, which means that an emotional response, especially with repetition, becomes ingrained and habitual. This is part of the law of *karma* (Pāli : *kamma*), a word which has more than one meaning. Prince Siddhārtha defined *karma* as mental activity (*cetanā*)[5] which leaves a lasting trace. Put neurologically, this means that everything we think or do involves electrical activity in the nervous system (*cetanā*) which may produce a lasting change there. Such a change in the nervous system is the physical basis of learning. *So Prince Siddhārtha is saying that mental disorder is a learned emotional habit.*

This conclusion is exactly the same as the one reached by the behaviourist school of psychotherapy, which also defines neurosis as a learned emotional habit. It is to the behaviourists that the Buddhists should look for modern parallels with their theory, not Freud and the psychoanalytical school. Indeed, the *Nidāna* analysis of the process of learning emotional habits has been borne out by the experimental work of the father of behaviourism, the great Russian physiologist, Ivan Pavlov. Pavlov's dogs exhibited the *Nidāna* process of a stimulus giving rise to feeling—either directly or by association—and feeling giving rise to an emotional response, which is learned and repeated whenever that stimulus occurs again. Prince Siddhārtha said, and the behaviourists have echoed him, that all of us exhibit this process most of the time.

But Prince Siddhārtha goes further than the behaviourists and avoids the erros into which they have fallen. For example, by a misinterpretation of Darwin's theory of evolution, the behaviourists have classified emotional responses to some stimuli as healthy and to others as unhealthy. The healthy responses are 'adaptive' and the unhealthy responses are 'unadaptive' to the environment, including the social environment. As a result of this unscientific classification, the behaviourist theory of mental disorder has degenerated into a theory of social adjustment, and has been rightly rejected by the thinking public. Prince Siddhārtha does not make this false and narrow division of emotional responses into healthy and unhealthy; he holds that *all* emotional responses to *all* stimuli are mentally unhealthy. This position prevents the Buddhist theory of mental disorder from ever becoming a tool for social adjustment and control.

Prince Siddhārtha's theory is altogether more comprehensive than that of the behaviourists. For one thing, it recognizes the universality of mental disorder. We all suffer from it, not just those who have been referred to a psychiatrist or who have been legally defined as 'insane'. And for another, it gives full prominence to the role of conceptualization. It recognizes that we are all scientists and all suffer the same difficulties in interpreting sense experience conceptually.

The whole *Nidāna* theory is summarized in the tenth *nidāna* of *bhava*. *Bhava*, which means 'life' or 'existence', arises because of learned emotional habits (*upādāna*). It is *bhava* which is said to be a wheel—the Wheel of Life. 'Life' is a process of moving from sense experience to the conceptual interpretation, and back again, not in a controlled fashion, but under the impetus of learned emotional responses to sense stimuli and concepts. What we are today is the sum total of all these emotional habits, which we have acquired haphazardly and willy-nilly from our earliest infancy. *It is these accumulated emotional habits, not any ego, which give rise to our compulsive behaviour and to the babble in our heads, which drives round the Wheel of Life to make saṃsāra, the world of ceaseless mental turmoil in which we live and suffer.*

I hope this comparison of the Wheel of Life with modern science has shown that the early Buddhists were right in insisting that it is the central theory of Buddhism. Established upon a modern scientific philosophy of cause and effect, and introduced with the bold claim that everything is accessible to scientific study, it sets out, in the *Nidānas*, two great theories. The first is the theory of reincarnation, which is only now beginning to be studied seriously by Western science. The second is the theory of mental disorder.

This magnificent analysis rejects the notion of an ego; instead it traces mental suffering to the two roots of ignorance and emotion. It describes the process of conceptualizing sense experience, showing that it is circular i.e., the Wheel of Life, which we can now (hypothetically) trace to a neural circuit in the brain. It shows how emotional habits are formed and holds that it is *emotional habits and not an ego*, which drive round the Wheel of Life continually. The modern Western equivalent of the *Nidānas* is *not* the theories of Freud and his school, but those of the behaviourist school, based on the pioneering work of Ivan Pavlov. Despite this recent progress, I think it is no exaggeration to say that Prince Siddhārtha's *Nidāna* theory is still, East or West, the very best theory of mental disorder available.

REFERENCES

1. Murti, T. R. V. : *The Central Philosophy of Buddhism.* George Allen and Unwin. 1960. P. 121.
2. Majjhima-Nikāya III.63. Saṃyutta-Nikāya II. Ch. XIII. 3, 21, 4, 37 and 7, 61. The translation is from *What the Buddha Taught,* by Walpola Rahula. Gordon Fraser, Bedford. 1967.
3. Christmas Humphreys : *A Western Approach to Zen.* George Allen and Unwin. 1971. Ch.3.
4. Saṃyutta-Nikāya II. 213. Pāli Text Society.
5. Aṅguttara-Nikāya III. 415. P. T. S.

SCIENCE AND THE WAY TO NIRVĀṆA

by

GERALD DU PRÉ

The way to enlightenment and *nirvāṇa* is the Noble Eightfold Path, the fourth of the Four Noble Truths; the most important section of this path is *bhāvanā* or meditation.

Inevitably, over the last two and a half thousand years, *Buddhist meditation* has diversified as it has spread from one culture to another; it has become encrusted with ceremony and tradition. As a result, there are today a bewildering array of Buddhist meditations; the proponents of any one of them often lay great stress on minor aspects so as to differentiate their tradition from the others. Despite this variety, most Buddhist schools still succeed in getting people enlightened.

In the Abhidhammas, Buddhist writers have made a detailed analysis of meditation into its constituent parts. It is an excellent analysis—methodical and based upon direct experience of what is described. Modern science can take this as a basis, can add to it and relate it to modern knowledge of the nervous system. This will give the would-be Buddhist meditators an objective criterion against which to judge the value of this or that technique or tradition. In time, it should also give rise to such a specifically Western form of Buddhist meditation as is thoroughly at home in the modern world.

The first thing a novice meditator has to tackle is the *posture*. There are a great many of these, a number of them very painful, and some of them almost certainly bad for the legs. Different schools prescribe different postures and emphasize seemingly minor points such as the position of the hands. Which posture should the Westerner choose?

Fortunately, the Japanese scientists have done some research on some of the postures used in Buddhist meditation. Out of these, they have found that the full-lotus is the most stable.[1] They have also reached the conclusion that no one posture is of vital importance in meditation. What matters, they have found, is the mental state of the meditator;[2] this view is also found in the Abhidhamma analysis. It appears that any posture which allows the meditator to be both relaxed and alert will do. Scientific findings like these can save Western meditators from quite unnecessary bodily contortions and the agony which goes with them!

In Buddhist meditation, there is no rigid *breath control*, as is there in some Hindu meditations. Instead, the Buddhist meditator breathes naturally, using the breath, if at all, simply as something to concentrate on or be mindful of. The Japanese scientists have studied this aspect of Buddhist meditation too and have found that as meditation proceeds, breathing becomes slower and lesser air is breathed in,[3] that breathing is done mainly from the abdomen;[4] this is the normal sort of breathing if the body is pleasantly relaxed.

What emerges so far, then, is that the first fundamental of Buddhist meditation is not the posture or breathing, but *bodily relaxation*.

The second fundamental, found in all Buddhist meditation, is *non-reaction*. The meditator does not react physically or mentally to any stimulus or, if he does react, he does so slowly and deliberately. All automatic responses are checked. Since emotion plays an important part in giving rise to physical and mental activity, this non-reaction is largely a matter of avoiding emotional responses. The Abhidhamma writers speak of the meditator cultivating non-desire or non-attachment (*alobha*) and non-ill will (*adosa*; Sanskrit: *adveṣa*) and equanimity (*upekkhā*; Sanskrit: *upekṣā*).

Inhibiting emotional responses is scientifically known as desensitization and is now-a-days used in behaviour therapy as a cure for phobias. (This therapy, called systematic desensitization, is described in my article 'Buddhism and Psychology'.)

How this process works neurologically is not yet clear. There are various hypotheses which are in the process of being tested experimentally.[5]

However, application of desensitization therapy has already provided some practical information. For example, in this therapy, while relaxing, one deliberately concentrates on objects which normally evoke an emotional response. In Buddhist meditation, at the moment, these objects are mostly left to arise of their own accord. It could be that they should be more deliberately picked as subjects for meditation. Also, these 'emotional objects' must be experienced at first in a mild form, and then, step by step, in stronger forms. Once again, in Buddhist meditation, this gradual escalation of the intensity with which emotional objects arise is left largely to chance. Once again, it could be that a more deliberate grading of intensity should take place. In desensitization therapy, at each level of intensity, relaxation must be maintained and only when this is done with ease, should the next level be attempted. According to one theory at least, to move on too quickly and thereby lose relaxation and succumb to an emotional response, serves to *reinforce* emotional responses, not inhibit them. This echoes the emphasis in Buddhist meditation on the importance of maintaining a relaxed and non-reacting state. It also shows that if non-reaction cannot be maintained, it is probably particularly important that meditation should stop at once. In many ways like this, work on desensitization therapy, both practical and theoretical, can provide important scientific information about Buddhist meditation, and help to make it more efficient.

The third fundamental of all types of Buddhist meditation is *attention*. It is likely that this aspect of meditation is a fairly simple process of learning. It is training the attention faculty of the brain, just as one would train any other faculty of the body in order to gain a skill.

The Abhidhamma account is very clear. The meditator begins with the ordinary faculty of attention (*manasikāra*; Sanskrit: *manaskāra*). He deliberately applies it to the object of his meditation, whereupon it becomes applied attention (*vitakka*; Sanskrit: *vitarka*). With training, the meditator learns to sustain attention (*vicāra*) for long periods of time. Thus attention which is found in even the most advanced stages of meditation is none other than ordinary attention, trained to a high degree.

Attention meditation is of two main sorts, according to whether the object of meditation is *one* or *many*. This is the basic Buddhist division of meditation into *Samatha* and *Vipassanā*.

Attention focused on one thing only is called in the Abhidhammas *one-pointed attention* or *ekāggatā* (Sanskrit: *ekāgratā*). It is said to be synonymous with *samādhi* or concentration, and also with right concentration in the Eightfold Path. The Buddhist meditator may not always be aware that he is doing this sort of meditation. It crops up in Tibetan Buddhism as 'visualizations' and throughout the Mahāyāna schools, as meditations on *mantras*, such as the invocation to Amida Buddha used in the Pure Land School of Japan. In short, any meditation which focuses attention on one thing, to the exclusion of all others, is one-pointed meditation. In Hinduism this meditation can be an end in itself. The meditator gains composure of mind by maintaining fixed attention on one thing and retreating into a trance. If a sudden tragedy strikes anyone in ordinary daily life, he stifles mental suffering by slipping quickly into this meditation, locking his attention on to his object of meditation and keeping it there. The Abhidhammas make it very clear that this is only the tranquillizing of mental confusion, not a proper cure, which is probably the reason why it is called *samatha*, or tranquillity (i.e., tranquillization). So long as meditation lasts, unhealthy mental factors such as desire and anger are inhibited, but the moment it comes to an end, they all arise again. Modern science has also found that mere disuse is not sufficient to eradicate emotional responses.[6]

On the other hand, one-pointed meditation is used in Buddhism simply as a technique for developing attention. As such, modern science should be able to contribute to its efficiency in many ways. Research on attention could probably decide which objects are best to focus attention on—visual or auditory, simple or complex, and so on. Research on learning in general could decide the optimum length of time for doing this meditation and the frequency and duration of rest periods. Technology might even be able to provide a system whereby a bell sounds when attention strays, a system which could prove more efficient than even the most watchful of Zen masters!

Once developed, attention can then be used in meditation proper.[7] True or genuine Buddhist meditation is called insight meditation, or *vipassanā*. According to the Abhidhammas, *vipassanā* begins with the Four Foundations of Mindfulness (*sati-paṭṭhāna*; Sanskrit: *smṛti-upasthāna*). Mindfulness (*sati*; Sanskrit: *smṛti*) is yet another term for attention and it is applied, in the first foundation, to the body, in the second to pain and pleasure, in the third to states of mind and in the fourth, to the contents of mind. Taken together, the Four Foundations cover almost everything which could possibly arise in experience. *Thus in vipassanā, attention is applied, not to just one thing, but to everything.* Attention is broadened out until it becomes what Trungpa calls 'panoramic awareness'.[8]

This sort of meditation is no longer merely a subject for scientific examination. Instead, *it is scientific examination itself*! The meditator is training himself to observe fully and accurately in a detached and unemotional way, just as a scientist strives to do. Again, like a scientist, he observes direct experience, and does so without assumptions, without interference, and strictly in the present. What the meditator *doesn't* do is to conceptualize his observation, because he is observing experience as a whole. Consequently concepts, ideas, theories are all on the same footing as sense perceptions; they also are just material for detached observation.

There is a second stage of mindfulness, however, which is called 'clear comprehension' (*sampajañña*),[9] and which moves on from bare attention to an *active investigation* of the object of meditation. The meditator now observes objects of experience in the light of Buddhist doctrines. In the first Foundation of Mindfulness, for example, the body is viewed as ever-changing, without any enduring essence or soul, and as the cause of present suffering. This process is repeated in the remaining three foundations, and also in the third, fourth and sixth 'Purities' (*Viśuddhi*). The sixth *Viśuddhi* is divided up into nine kinds of insight (*vipassanā-ñāna*) which is meditation on the arising, passing away and disappearance of things, and the futility of trying to cling to them.

It is easy to misunderstand this kind of meditation as a sort of self-imposed brain-washing, an auto-indoctrination in a set of religious dogmas in an attempt to eradicate doubt. In religions which demand complete faith in dogmas, such as Roman Catholicism, this may actually be the case. But it is not so in Buddhism. On the contrary, the meditator is actually using a form of *experimental method.* He is adopting Buddhist doctrines and is *testing them against experience.*

Observing the contents of experience with attention and detachment, he discovers for himself that they are indeed changing all the time. Try as he may, he cannot find any evidence of an everlasting core or soul in himself or in any other object or process. In the *vipassanā-ñānas*, the meditator comes to *see* that what he took to be his body and mind are simply a stream of experiences in which perceptions and ideas continually arise, fade and disappear. Since things do fade and disappear, it is clearly dangerous, vain and an utter waste of time to cling to them. He comes to know by direct experience that the one and only way to escape from this life of clinging to insubstantial things is to give up emotional desires and aversions and maintain, instead, equanimity towards all things. Each new meditator, in the process of meditation, can repeat the Buddha's own observations and test for himself the Buddha's doctrines. This investigation of Buddhist theory and philosophy in the light of personal experience is called the development of wisdom or *prajñā* (Pāli : *paññā*); it is the fourth and last fundamental Buddhist meditation. In Buddhism there are two definitions of wisdom which, on closer examination, turn out to be merely two stages.

In the Abhidhammas of the early schools descriptions of *paññā* make clear that it means scientific knowledge. In more recent Theravādin commentaries, it is specifically compared to the sort of knowledge possessed by a chemist, who knows the chemical properties and constituents of everything he sees. In the same way, while observing the contents of his mind, the meditator considers the physical constituents of his body and the causes of mental events. We often hear it said that Western culture, particularly science, has led Westerners away from the wisdom which is acquired in meditation. But it is quite the opposite! The native scientific attitude of Westerners actually gives them an *advantage* so far as this first sort of wisdom is concerned. After four hundred years of science and two hundred years of atheism, most Westerners cannot believe in an everlasting soul even if they *want* to ! And, after Freud, they hardly need to be told that mental events have a cause. Nor, in the age of biochemistry, is it news to them that the body is a self-organizing collection of molecules.

Indeed, some aspects of Abhidhamma analysis can now be replaced by more modern scientific information. For example, meditation on the constituents of the body (*eka* or *dhātuvavatthāna*), which is found in both *samatha* and *vipassanā*, should no longer analyse the body into the four elements of the primitive Buddhist physics, but into the modern elements of carbon, oxygen, nitrogen, and so on.

Some psychotherapists might question whether such knowledge really helps us to solve mental problems. I think it does. We acquire most of our deep-seated fears and phobias when we are very young; this is when we are most ignorant. If we fall into a river as an adult, we do not acquire a fear of water, because we know enough to blame, not the water, but our own clumsiness. As scientific knowledge eliminates ignorance, so it eliminates fear. The doctor is not afraid of illness and death, because he knows their causes and consequences.

The weakness of the early Buddhist view of wisdom is that it seems to limit it to certain Buddhist doctrines, and, despite protestations to the contrary by the Theravādins, it seems to make them into dogmas. Revising Buddhist doctrines in the light of the latest scientific knowledge improves the situation. However, the fact is that any knowledge, however sound, however scientific, will be incomplete and open to error and subject to change. Consequently, the Mahāyāna school has classed all Buddhist doctrines as part of relative truth and has given wisdom (*prajñā*), a more profound meaning. It has defined wisdom as seeing the ultimate basis of all knowledge. It means seeing that everything is *experience*, and seeing experience *just as it is, in its true suchness*, without the intervention of any conceptualization, however profound or subtle it may be. Intellectually, this is the Buddhist philosophy of science. Experienced directly, it is total liberation from the darkness of ignorance.

The early Buddhist and Mahāyāna views in fact describe two stages on the path of wisdom. The early schools such as the Theravāda stress the *way* to ultimate wisdom which is still within the world of relative truth, while the Mahāyāna stresses the ultimate wisdom itself.

In this brief survey, combining and comparing the Abhidhamma analysis with modern scientific research, we have been able to pick out *four 'pillars' of Buddhist meditation. They are muscular relaxation, non-reaction, attention and wisdom.* These, it seems, are the 'active ingredients' of meditation and can serve as a touchstone by which to judge the nature and value of the meditation practices of any particular Buddhist tradition.

And *nirvāṇa*, it seems, is the fullest possible development of these four. In *nirvāṇa*, they are no longer deliberately applied; they operate naturally and, at every moment of day and night. The nervous system is both relaxed and ready to spring into action whenever it is required. The emotional responses of desire, aversion and fear no longer arise or, if they do, they are instantly noted by the ever-alert attention and checked. In place of these old emotions, there is the positive emotion of Buddhist *compassion*—an all-embracing love without desire.

These aspects of *nirvāṇa* are still within the realm of relative truth and so, are open to scientific investigation. But *nirvāṇa* is not just a state of mental health, a particular state of the brain. *The fourth fundamental of wisdom transforms nirvāṇa from a psychological state into complete transcendence.*[10] By wisdom the enlightened person *sees* that the whole material world, with all its laws, is just a *theoretical model*; theories are words and figures, and words and figures are just sights and sounds, and sights and sounds are *actual* experience. Since actual experience contains all theories, it is itself beyond all theorizing and all investigation. This is why the enlightened person is no longer subject to rebirth, having shattered the chain of causation. And this is how *nirvāṇa* ultimately transcends psychology and the brain, and the whole of science, and the whole universe to its farthest end.

REFERENCES

1. Ryutaro Ikegami. Psychological Study of Zen Posture, in *Psychological Studies on Zen*, edited by Yoshiharu Akishige. Circulated in photocopy.

2. Suzuki, T. *Electroencephalographic study during Zen practice.* Proc. 15th Convention of J-EEG-S, 1966, 28. Quoted by Akishige. Ch. 1. *Ibid.*

3. Hiromoto Matsumoto. *A Psychological Study of the Relation Between Respiratory Function and Emotion. Ibid.*
4. Yoshiharu Akishige. *A Historical Survey of the Psychological Studies on Zen. Ibid.*
5. Beech, H. R. *Changing Man's Behaviour*, Pelican 1969. Ch. 9. for a review of these theories.
6. Jones, M. C. *The Elimination of Children's Fears.* Journal of Experimental Psychology, 7, 383-90. (1924).
7. This distinction between the *training* of attention and the *application* of attention in meditation is made by Christmas Humphreys, in *Concentration and Meditation.* Buddhist Society Publication. London. 1935.
8. Chögyam Trungpa. *Cutting Through Spiritual Materialism.* Watkins. London. 1973. Pages 167, 168.
9. Nyanaponika Thera. *The Heart of Buddhist Meditation.* Rider & Co. London. 1962. Ch. 2.
10. Rune Johansson. *The Psychology of Nirvāṇa.* George Allen and Unwin. 1969.

In this detailed collation of descriptions of *nirvāṇa* in the Pāli Canon, he finds that it is described both as a psychological state and as transcendence.

SCIENTIFIC BUDDHISM

by

GERALD DU PRÉ

The comparison between Buddhism and science is not just an academic matter. Western culture is deeply divided because its traditional religion is incompatible with science. For over four hundred years, Christianity has waged war on science and lost every engagement. Today science lies at the heart of our culture and has become an irresistible force, while Christianity has been pushed into a corner.

Even with the omnipotence of science and almost complete disappearance of religion, it seems that this division will not end, as many people had thought it would. Atheism has proved to be inadequate. Science without a transcendent aspect seems cold, heartless and mundane, and it is becoming clear that transcendence is a basic human need. So it is that some twentieth century men and women are rejecting science and are searching for the meaning of life in religion, dogmatic Marxism, the occult and in 'alternative' ways of life.

It is a genuine search, but for the most part, it is wrongly directed because by seeking an *alternative* to science, these people are only deepening that fatal division between religion and science which is the root of the problem. What is required is a bringing together of religion and science so that religion becomes scientific and science becomes transcendent. Christianity is completely unsuitable for this task. I believe that we have the answer to the problem in Buddhism.

In Buddhism, science and the search for transcendence are brought together. Buddhism can heal our culture of its painful rift; at the same time it can also bring together East and West. Buddhism and science united could form the foundation of a unified world culture.

This is no mere academic matter, but a powerful vision of the future. I believe this is the future which lies before Western Buddhism. However, it is very easy to speak in this bold and sweeping manner. If these assertions are to have any value, they must be supported by hard facts. What specific factual justification is there for calling Buddhism 'scientific'?

Buddhism is a scientific religion because it is based upon direct experience. It is empirical. This is stressed by practically every writer on Buddhism and is not really a controversial statement at all. Prince Siddhārtha, the Buddha, tried every method and theory available in his search for enlightenment; his teachings are based on his own authentic experience of what actually works. Through mindfulness, the Buddhist meditator learns how to make scientific observation—detached, accurate, without assumptions or interference, and strictly in the present. He repeats the Buddha's own observations, and by active investigation, he tests the Buddha's teachings against his own experience.

Consequently, in Buddhism, there is no divine god, saviour or authority. There are no dogmas, and so no faith to accept them. It is these things—divine authority, dogma and blind faith—which make Christianity and virtually every other religion incompatible with science. But Buddhism does not have them. Instead, it honours the same authority as science, that of immediate experience, observed with unqualified attention and emotional detachment.

In fact Prince Siddhārtha may well be the founder of scientific psychology. I have argued this point in 'Buddhism and Science'[1] and 'Buddhism and Psychology',[2] and I think that the matter is worth pursuing further. The West has got so used to being in the forefront of every area of science that it has assumed that it has invented even psychology. But in this area, if in no other, I think the Buddhist East has every reason to contest the claim.

If, in due course, this point was conceded, it would mean that the whole history of psychology would have to be rewritten. But is this as far as it goes? Is the scientific nature of Buddhism now a matter of history only, Buddhist theory just part of the archaeology of science, like alchemy and phrenology?

Up till now, most attempts at comparing Buddhist theories with the theories of modern science have laboured under what I feel is a fatal misconception. In the West, we are still prone to take a metaphysical view of psychology, seeing the mind as a sort of ghostly semi-material, semi-spiritual thing, never quite one thing or the other. As a result, popular psychology, such as that of Jung and his followers, persistently ignores research on the nervous system, including the brain and talks in very loose terms about the 'mind' as if it led an independent existence. Simply because Buddhist psychology too doesn't mention the nervous system, it has been automatically compared with this popular and largely unscientific kind of Western psychology. Yet Buddhist psychology quite clearly rejects the soul-like mind upon which this Western psychology is based. And whereas this Western psychology knows about the nervous system, it deliberately chooses to ignore it. On the other hand, the Buddhist psychologists make no mention of the nervous system because they know nothing at all about it and are loath to speculate about what they do not know. If they had had our modern knowledge, I am sure that they would have described much of the Abhidhamma psychology in terms of the activity of nerve cells.

This is just my opinion which, of course, cannot now be proved either way. What is definite is that the Buddhist psychological theory comes alive and makes sense only when it is detached from psychoanalysis and Jung and other fringe psychology and is teamed up instead with modern neurobiology. *Then* the *Skandhas* make sense, meditation becomes accessible, and the *Nidānas* leap forward into the twentieth century.

When the *Skandhas* are translated into neurological terms, they turn out to be a remarkably accurate account of how the contact of sense stimuli with sense receptors gives rise to perception and experience. I have given an account of this in 'Science and the *Skandhas*'.[3] The *Skandhas* may not have anything new to offer to us today, but they still provide a sounder theoretical basis than many modern schools of psychology possess.

When the second half of the *Nidānas* is considered from the neurological point of view, it turns out to be a precursor of Ivan Pavlov and the Behaviourist School of Psychology. Like them, it defines neuroses as learned emotional habits. Many people are mildly appalled at the clinical approach of Pavlov and his followers, and are more than mildly disturbed by the fact that modern psychiatry is usually no better than an agent of repressive governments—capitalist or communist—in its work of enforcing social conformity. To link Buddhism with such schools and people seems most inappropriate.

But it is the sick who need a physician ! Behaviour therapy is going astray because it lacks that vision of mental health and liberation which only Buddhism can give it. Instead of setting up Buddhist therapy in *contrast* to behaviour therapy, we must try to *unite* the two. Behaviour therapy can bring to Buddhism the benefits of modern science, while Buddhism can change behaviour therapy from a tool of oppression into a way of liberation.

Does this sound too ambitious ? I don't think so. The *Nidāna* theory, taken as a whole, describes mental disorder as the linking of emotional habits with the conceptualisation of sense experience; this causes circular neural activity which is extremely difficult to stop or even control. I have dealt with this in 'Science and the Wheel of Life'.[4] If the West has produced a better theory of mental disorder, I have yet to discover it.

More important than even this is the fact that Buddhism has a *cure* for mental disorder ! *Nirvāṇa*, the state of enlightenment, is the state of complete mental health and liberation. In the West, we have an organisation which is trying to set a standard of mental health. Are the members of that organisation aware that Buddhism has not only laid down these standards already, but has actually produced living embodiments of them in the form of enlightened men and women ? Is Western psychiatry aware that living ideals of mental health are today walking the streets of our Western cities ? It seems that they are not and I think it is about time Buddhism made them aware of it. Of course, they may question whether *nirvāṇa* is really all that which the Buddhists claim for it. In that case, they have only to make scientific tests on enlightened people. This is quite feasible, and indeed work of this sort has already begun in Japan.

The way to enlightenment is Buddhist meditation. At the moment, a Westerner who embarks on Buddhist meditation has no objective criterion by which to evaluate what he is doing.

Some people make a virtue of this. In the East, they say, the meditator is happy to do just as he is told, and does not ask the reason why. Knowledge *about* meditation, they say, will only distract by encouraging intellectualisation of what one is doing. On the contrary, I believe that *lack* of knowledge is a distraction for a Westerner. At the moment he is continually bothered by the thoughts: 'What am I trying to do in meditation ? Am I wasting my time ? Am I making any progress' ? If he knew the answers to these questions, *then* he would *stop* thinking about meditation and would instead throw himself wholeheartedly into *doing* it.

These questions *can* be answered when Buddhist meditation is viewed in a neurological way. Meditation is then seen as a learning process—the process of *learning* enlightenment. I have dealt with this in 'Science and the Way to *Nirvāṇa*',[5] where I have provisionally analysed Buddhist meditation into the four fundamental elements of muscular relaxation, non-reaction, attention and wisdom. Any technique of Buddhist meditation should consist of the practice of one or more of these four, and with the help of an analysis of this sort, the meditator can know exactly what he is trying to do. He knows whether he is trying to relax, 'unlearn' emotional reactions, train his attention or gain wisdom. In the first three of these at least, it is not too difficult to check how far he has progressed.

Expressing Buddhist meditation in neurological terms also makes it possible to relate it specifically to modern methods of psychotherapy, as I have tried to show in 'Buddhism and Psychotherapy'.[6] For example, the non-reaction aspect of Buddhist meditation can be related to the behaviour therapy known as systematic desensitisation. It is this sort of exact, practical comparison which will enable Buddhist meditational techniques to transform modern psychotherapy into a way of liberation. On the other hand, the application of scientific method to Buddhist meditation can make it progressively still more effective and efficient.

These are some of the positive ways in which Buddhism and science can come together and enrich each other. But many people who have read this far will probably be saying: 'Yes, there may be some element of truth in what you say, but by discussing Buddhism in terms of the nervous system, aren't you reducing it to materialism, to which Buddhism is fundamentally opposed?'

Buddhism is indeed opposed to materialism. In particular, the Mahāyāna School is opposed to it; it is also opposed to idealism. But while rejecting materialism, the Mahāyāna philosophy does not reject science, or the nervous system. On the contrary, the Mahāyāna philosophy, the central and most profound philosophy of Buddhism, is a thoroughgoing philosophy of science, probably the oldest and the finest philosophy of science in the world !

The basis of the whole Mahāyāna philosophy is the distinction made by Nāgārjuna between absolute and relative truth. On the face of it, this doesn't seem likely to be a very helpful or original distinction. Every religion or metaphysical philosophy tends to make a distinction between divine and mundane truth, or between higher and lower truth. But Nāgārjuna's distinction goes a great deal deeper than any of these.

It does so because his *absolute truth* is not a body of doctrines, but points to *total actual experience*. This does not mean *an* experience, such as one might have in moments of ecstasy, neither is it the *concept* of 'experience', to be used in a psychological discussion. Instead, it is the totality of experience now this minute, the *direct* experience of sight, sound, taste, smell, touch and conceptual thought.

Similarly, *relative truth* is not any particular doctrine or body of knowledge. Instead, it is a general term covering any truth which is expressed in words or numbers, or in any other kind of symbols. The whole philosophy is a philosophy of science because by saying that relative truth is based upon absolute truth, it is saying that theories must be based upon direct and total experience. Relative truth means empirical truth. I have discussed this philosophy, and its consequences, in 'The Buddhist Philosophy of Science'.[7]

The body of Buddhist theory which we have considered above, the *Skandhas* and *Nidānas*, was worked out by the early Buddhist schools (such as the Sarvāstivāda and the Theravāda) scientifically—that is, it was based upon direct experience. But once laid down, the theory began to be considered settled and unchangeable. The Mahāyāna philosophy attacked this new dogmatic attitude and insisted that every word of Buddhist theory was only relative truth, not absolute. But the early Buddhist schools did not accept this criticism, and hence, the Mahāyāna School went on to concern itself almost entirely with the absolute truth.

Thus it has been left to the West to develop and systematize relative truth, in the form of science. Today, thanks to the experimental method, modern science is the finest body of relative truth the world has ever seen.

So, far from being opposed to science, the Mahāyāna philosophy embraces science. Further, far from declaring Buddhist theory and science incompatible, it brackets them together, since they are both equally relative truth—that is, both are conceptualisations of experience.

And since this is so, to speak of Buddhist theory in terms of the nervous system is not to reduce it to materialism. The nervous system, like any other aspect of Buddhist or scientific theory, is a *conceptual model*, a verbal description of experience. Matter is a word ! To say that the nervous system is material, and that matter is ultimate, would be to say that words can express absolute truth, which they cannot. It is the actual experience which is ultimately real, while the 'material world' is just a lot of words !

It is this Mahāyāna philosophy of science, far more profound than anything we have in the West, which can make modern science transcendent. It can do so by pointing out that it is not just *sense* experience which is the ultimate truth, but *total* experience. Concepts are not only *based* upon sense experience, but are bits of experience *themselves. Concepts too are experience.* And so the whole conceptual edifice of science, the whole story of the basic constituents of matter, the evolution of life, and the rise and fall of galaxies, can only exist in actual experience here and now !

This viewpoint may seem hard to grasp and may seem to lead to confusion rather than transcendence. Yet it is not obscure or abstruse; it is difficult to grasp only because it is so obvious and open to view. It is understood, and transcendence is realised, not by thinking about it, but by *looking*, which is the first rule of both science and Buddhism. And we learn how to look in meditation.

In this series on Buddhism and science,[8] I have packed in a great deal of material, probably far too much. Yet there is so much more which should have been mentioned ! However, I hope I have at least said enough to show that it is possible to combine Buddhism and science at every level—practical, theoretical and philosophical.

This is not just an academic matter. The bringing together of Buddhist and scientific theory can change psychotherapy into a way of liberation, while the Mahāyāna philosophy can make the whole weighty edifice of science light and airy and transcendent. In our culture, torn in two by the incompatibility between our religion and our science, Buddhism can bring unity and peace.

During this century, a great deal of work has been done for uniting the religions of the world, with the praiseworthy object of discovering what they have in common, and for promoting tolerance among them. However, this has not led to a revival of religion, because what most religions have in common is faith, dogma, divine scriptures and the deities, all of which make them incompatible with science. Buddhism (along with Taoism) is the great exception to this, for it is not a faith, has no dogma or divine authority of its own and does not accept the validity of anyone else's.

I don't believe that we should be trying to unite Buddhism with other religions. This only leads to confusion. Instead, we should be striving to unite Buddhism and science, so as to produce a religion of science for our modern world. Scientific Buddhism will dispel confusion by clarifying and unifying Buddhist practice and theory and making it an effective stepping-stone to enlightenment for Westerners.

Many people believe that there must eventually arise a specifically Western form of Buddhism suitable to Western needs. In my opinion, this Western branch of Buddhism will be Scientific Buddhism. I hope this series of articles has gone some way towards laying the foundation for this school and that people who share my hopes for it will unite to make it grow and flourish.

REFERENCES

1. *The Middle Way.* Vol. 51, No. 3. November 1976.
2. *Ibid.* Vol. 52, No. 2. August 1977.
3. *Ibid.* Vol. 52, No. 3. November 1977.
4. *Ibid.* Vol. 52, No. 4. February 1978.
5. *Ibid.* Vol. 53, No. 1. May 1978.
6. *Ibid.* Vol. 51, No. 4. February 1977.
7. *Ibid.* Vol. 52, No. 1. May 1977.
8. *Ibid.* From Vol. 51, No. 3. November 1976 to Vol. 53, No. 2. August 1978.

CONTRIBUTORS

Late Dr. K. N. Jayatilleke, B.A. (Ceylon), M.A. (Cantab), Ph. D. (London). Professor of Buddhist Philosophy, University of Sri Lanka (Ceylon).

Dr. Robert F. Spencer, M.A., Ph.D., Professor of Philosophy, University of Minnesota.

Venerable Nanajivako of Sri Lanka, a Bhikkhu (monk) well known for his Buddhist scholarship.

Dr. Shanti Tayal, M.D. A practising psychotherapist, educated both in India and the U.S.A.

Upasaka Wu Shu (Dr. Loo Yung Taung), Ph.D., Physicist, now living in a Buddhist monastery in Hong Kong.

Dr. U. Aung Thein, Ph.D. A well known biochemist of Burma.

Mr. Frederick M. Davis, B.A., M.A. (U.C.). A well known contributor to Buddhist Journals.

Dr. Buddhadasa P. Kirthisinghe, B.Sc. (McGill), M.S. (W.S.U.), D.D. (H.C.), Buddha Dharma Śāstra Viśārada, General Secretary, Council on Asian Affairs, Representative of Mahā Bodhi Society of India and Ceylon, and of the World Fellowship of Buddhists (Bangkok) and Honorary Minister, American Buddhist Academy, New York City.

Mr. Gerald du Pré, B.A. (Nottingham), President, Scientific Buddhist Association, London.

INDEX